INTRODUCING BONSAI

INTRODUCING BONSAI

CHRISTIAN PESSEY
in association with Rémy Samson

HAMLYN

Produced by: Éditions Hespérides, 41, rue de la Chine, 75020 Paris
(Anne Laurence, Renée Meunier)
Photography: Christian Pessey except for:
Guy Casas: 53, 63 tr, br, 71 (except t), 77 r; Georges Papot: 34, 80, 26; Yves-André Robic
27 b, 36 t, c, 42, 43, 54, 63 bl, 65 cl, 103, 110.
Artwork: Jean-Marie Bévillard, Michel Blot, Brigitte Massot, Christian Pessey.
Photographic subjects taken from the collection of Rémy Samson, Châtenay-Malabry.

First published in 1989 by the Hamlyn Publishing Group Limited,
a division of the Octopus Publishing Group
Michelin House
81 Fulham Road
London SW3 6RB

Text and illustrations taken from the work
Les Bonsaï
© Bordas, Paris, 1985
Éditions Bordas
17 rue Rémy Dumoncel
75014 PARIS

Translated by Marion Godfrey

ISBN 0-600-56699-4 (h/b)
ISBN 0-600-56756-7 (p/b)

Produced by Mandarin Offset
Printed and bound in Hong Kong

CONTENTS

HOW TREES GROW

Although the cultivation of bonsai requires some highly specialized techniques, bonsai themselves are first and foremost just trees, and as such grow in much the same way as the trees in woods and forests. So it is a good idea to remind yourself what a tree is, the various parts of its anatomy, how a broad-leaved tree differs from a conifer and a deciduous one from an evergreen, and above all, what conditions favour its development. All of these elements are indispensable to growing bonsai successfully.

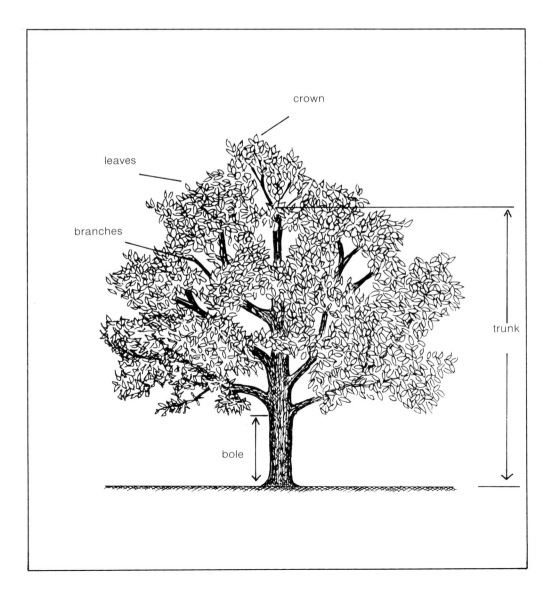

DEFINITION

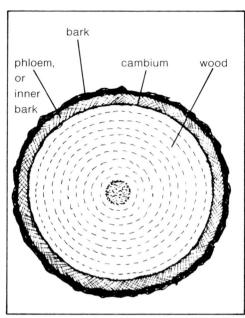

Section of trunk showing the different layers. The annual growth rings are clearly visible.

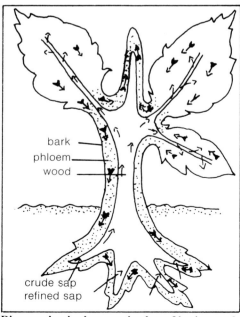

Diagram showing how sap circulates. Nutrients and water taken in through the roots rise within the tree, then sap returns to the roots carrying sugar.

Of all plants, trees live the longest, thanks to a permanent structure of trunk and branches, which ensures that the leaves, flowers and fruits are nourished. This rigid permanent structure provides for the tree's long life; it is made of that particularly resilient substance, wood. A section cut across the trunk of a tree will show several zones. These are, starting from the outer ring and working towards the centre: the bark, the phloem, the cambium layer and the true heartwood. The cambium layer produces the wood fibres and the vessels which carry sap upwards to the aerial parts of the tree. As the tree grows, these vessels become more numerous, with the new layers superimposed on the old, which gradually cease to play an active part in the life of the tree. In time, they harden to produce a substance which varies in its hardness according to the species: xylem, or wood. In this way, the annual life cycle of the tree produces successive layers of compressed xylem, clearly visible in a section of trunk. Each of these growth rings corresponds to one year in the life of a tree: so to ascertain the age of a tree, all you need do is count the rings.

In a well kept bonsai, the production of cambium is continuous and regular, as long as the water supply is constant. But a tree growing in its natural surroundings may have to cope with dramatic variations in climate which can considerably influence its growth.

Later in this book we shall see that a major preoccupation of the bonsai enthusiast is the thickening of the trunk. The art lies in allowing the trunk to thicken while miniaturizing the leaves and preserving the natural balance of the tree on a miniature scale. This can only be achieved by using artifice – wiring, and pruning the leaves, branches and roots. These methods can produce remarkable results.

ANATOMY OF A TREE

Whatever its species or variety, a tree has a particular anatomy, or structure, which is found in every example of its kind, regardless of age.

Underground parts

These consist of the roots of the tree which draw from the soil those substances which are vital to the tree's growth. A complex network of roots and rootlets ensures that the tree is at once firmly anchored and also fed. The capillary structure of the roots creates a continuous upward movement of water in the soil, making sure that the tree obtains all the substances it needs. The normal development of the aerial part of the tree (the focus of our interest) is linked to root development. If root growth is inhibited, the aerial part of the tree will stop growing and may even die, as a tree can only survive by growing. In bonsai, root growth is always restricted by the size of the container, which is why these trees must be regularly repotted.

The diagram shows how the roots relate to the branches and foliage of a tree in its natural state.

The root system is far less important in bonsai than it is in a tree allowed to grow naturally.

Aerial parts

These consist of the trunk and the branch system. From the base of the trunk to where the first branches grow is known as the bole and the top of the tree, at the tip of the last branch, is the crown. The branch system consists of the branches and their sub-divisions, the most slender of which produce the leaves. In nature, the development of these elements is directly related to the physical environment, such as sunlight, temperature and wind. The art of bonsai lies in limiting the growth of the tree, while artificially maintaining the natural look of its trunk and branch system. This is done by precise cutting, pruning and wiring techniques, which are described in detail later in this book.

Foliage

Leaves form an essential part of the tree and are directly involved in the tree's growth processes. In fact, they make possible the trapping of the sun's energy in the green chlorophyll they contain, a process vital to the development of all plant life. It is the leaves that absorb carbon dioxide from the atmosphere, a phenomenon which itself results from photosynthesis which takes place in sunlight. In darkness, particularly at night, the plant gives off the oxygen contained in the carbon dioxide. The carbohydrates necessary for growth are manufactured from water taken from the soil. The shape of leaves varies from one species to another, but there is a fundamental difference between the leaves of pines and similar trees and the leaves of other trees. The former are generally evergreen (that is, the leaves do not fall all at once in autumn – or indeed at any time of year), the latter are deciduous, since the leaves drop from the trees in autumn. But one should be careful of such generalizations since there are many exceptions to the rule.

It is desirable to distinguish the needles of the conifers from the leaves of other types of tree. Leaves are made up of a petiole or leaf stalk by which they are attached to the stem and a veined blade or lamina containing the cells which carry out photosynthesis.

blade

petiole

Most leaves are deciduous. The leaf itself is composed of the blade and the petiole, or stalk, which links it to the branch.

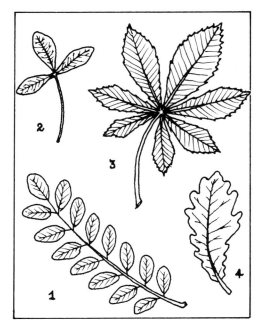

1. Pinnate leaf (false acacia) 2. Compound leaf with three leaflets (laburnum) 3. Palmate leaf (horse chestnut) 4. Simple leaf (oak)

Leaves may vary according to species and variety; they may be simple (the oak leaf, for example), multiple and compound (like the horse chestnut); they may be regular in shape, dentate or linear, ovate, lanceolate or cuneate, etc. A conifer needle is very simple in structure. Its main characteristic is its narrow, elongated shape tapering to a point (hence the name). Unlike a leaf blade of a typical broad-leaved tree which is generally very thin, the needle is fleshy and thick, making it very resilient. But like leaves, needles also provide for photosynthesis.

The needle-like leaf is a good example of the way in which the leaf has adapted to a dry, cold or hot climate, by restricting transpiration. Because a needle lasts for several years, the tree is released from the burden of forming a complete set of new leaves every year. But it should be noted that the needle's permanence is only relative, since they also eventually fall from the tree: a look under the nearest conifer will confirm this. Once fallen, all leaves start to decompose and help to form humus. In this way, some of the minerals drawn up by the roots are returned to the soil.

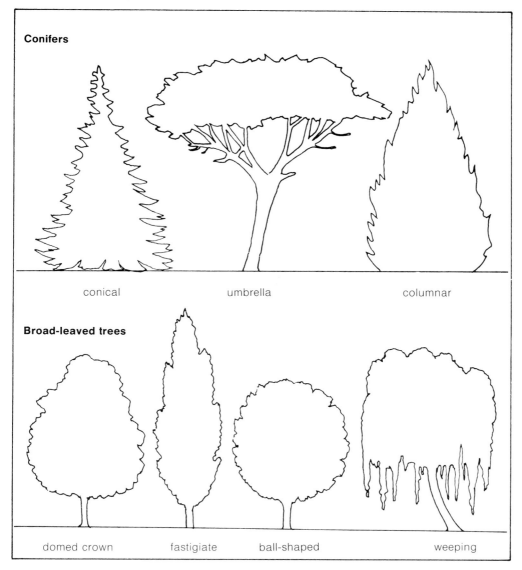

Conifers

conical   umbrella   columnar

Broad-leaved trees

domed crown   fastigiate   ball-shaped   weeping

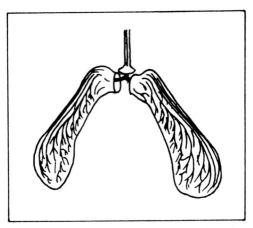

Elm, ash and maple produce winged fruits like this, called samaras.

The acorn, fruit and seed of the oak, is attached to the twig by a cupula.

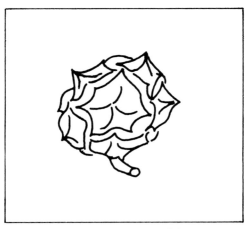

Some conifers, like the false cypress (*Chamaecyparis*) and juniper do not produce typical cones but round, scaly fruits.

Flowers and fruits

Almost all trees propagate themselves sexually from seeds, which develop as the result of the union of a male and a female cell. This union takes place within the flower, which is simply a leaf specially adapted for reproduction purposes. Seeds vary greatly in type and shape from tree to tree. For instance, they may take the form of a fleshy fruit whose pulp contains the seeds, or a protective nut, a berry, or an achene (dry, one-seeded fruit), or held within a cone in the case of a conifer. Reproductive cells are produced in the flower by specialized organs: the stamens produce male cells (pollen), while the pistil produces the female cells (ovules). Where stamens and pistils are present in the same flower, the plant is said to be hermaphrodite; otherwise it is unisexual. In hermaphrodite plants, pollen falls directly on to the pistil sheltered by the petals, thereby fertilizing the ovules. In unisexual plants, pollen must be conveyed from flower to flower by the wind or honey-gathering insects.

The most beautiful flowers are frequently found on monoecious plants, since the bright colours of the petals are designed to attract honey-gathering insects. The flowers of forest trees (as opposed to ornamental shrubs) are often lacking in colour, to the point of insignificance, hardly standing out from the leaves, since they are mainly adapted to wind pollination. Some plants bear flowers of one sex only, male or female (dioecious), others flowers of both sexes (monoecious), while some kinds have male, female and hermaphrodite flowers (polygamous).

Pollination produces seeds, which, after germinating in the earth will produce a new plant like its parent (unless the plant has been grafted). For successful germination, conditions, particularly humidity, heat and light must be favourable. The percentage of seeds which germinate in nature is very low, particularly in those trees whose seeds are small and without any food reserves.

CONDITIONS FOR DEVELOPMENT

Soil

While the physical properties of the soil provide a secure anchorage for a tree, it is the soil's chemical composition (itself linked to the physical structure) which enables the tree to develop and grow.

First and foremost, the roots draw water from the ground, vital to the process of photosynthesis already described. This water also contains essential mineral salts in dissolved form. These are sure to include nitrates, phosphates, potassium, calcium, magnesium and sulphur, as well as a number of metallic elements (or trace elements) like copper, zinc, boron, iron, manganese, molybdenum, etc. These mineral salts are transported to all parts of the plant by the sap.

The mineral salt requirement varies from plant to plant; this means that the nature of the soil governs the natural vegetation of a particular region. Where trees are grown in containers (bonsai trays or trees in tubs), the potting compost chosen should be adapted to the needs of the tree.

Exposure to light

As we have already seen, light is indispensable to the process of photosynthesis, without which the plant cannot develop. Exposure to light is often confused with exposure to sunlight, which is not the same thing at all. Some plants which require a great deal of light may suffer from prolonged exposure to the sun, whose hot rays may cause rapid dehydration of the plant.

All trees need light, but the amount and length of time may vary. In nature, a tree may 'choose' its exposure to light, to the extent that only plants exposed to a certain intensity of light will thrive. In bonsai cultivation, a choice must be made: whether to opt for one species rather than another to suit the location (for example, balcony or patio) or to select the exposure to suit the needs of the plant as in larger areas such as gardens, large terraces or balconies with different aspects.

Before you buy a bonsai tree, you must always find out the degree of exposure to light it requires.

Exposure to wind

This is important to the development of a tree in its natural surroundings, but less likely to affect artificially cultivated plants, particularly bonsai, which grow only in a strictly controlled indoor environment not subject to windy conditions. At the same time, one should not overlook the fact that wind may accentuate the ambient conditions. For example, a bonsai exposed to the sun will be more prone to dehydration if it is exposed to wind at the same time. By the same token wind increases the risk of frost in cold conditions.

Generally speaking, a bonsai should not be grown in a windy place, such as the edge of a balcony or terrace. Draughts should also be avoided, as these prejudice normal plant development. Of course, where bonsai are grown outside, their containers must be firmly anchored, so that they cannot be dislodged by a gust of wind.

Where bonsai are put on window or balcony ledges, the trays must be secured with steel wire. In some cases, the plants may have to be anchored or braced, which will also prevent them being forced out of shape by prevailing winds.

Climate

This mainly denotes the ambient conditions and in particular, the temperature and humidity (moisture taken in by the roots and present in the air). It goes without saying that the growth of any tree is directly linked to the climatic conditions. Everyone knows that tropical vegetation differs vastly from that of a temperate or cold climate.

A climate which is clement for most of the year, allows most species to grow. In some cases, human intervention may be needed, to water plants, for example, or protect them from frost, but most species can be grown in the soil outdoors without much difficulty. In bonsai, this applies to all species that come from cold, mountainous or temperate regions. Bonsai trees can and *should live outdoors*, provided the climatic conditions are not too harsh. In general this means where the temperature does not usually drop below −5°C (23°F). If it does (or just before), the bonsai should be moved indoors during the cold weather, or into a well-lit room, where the temperature never exceeds 10°C (50°F). If the atmos-

phere becomes warmer and the level of humidity drops very low, the plant is likely to die. A horticultural maximum-minimum thermometer is available which can be placed near your bonsai.

Only some types of tree from the tropics need to be or will tolerate being grown indoors at a high temperature, above 15°C (60°F). Provided the atmosphere is humid enough, the plant is watered frequently and the leaves are frequently misted with water, these tropical trees should survive.

These 'indoor' bonsai can almost be considered as house plants. Some of them are simply ordinary indoor plants treated as bonsai – plants like azaleas, fuchsias, and so on.

Some genuinely tropical plants can also be grown under glass and treated, shaped and trained like bonsai. This applies to some bamboos, which can produce some very interesting effects. The distinctive elegance of the date palm (*Phoenix dactylifera*) which grows as a house plant to a height of 3 m (10 ft) or more but can be reduced to about 30 cm (1 ft), is also worth mentioning.

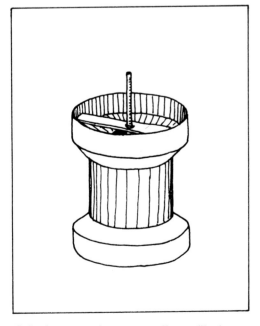

The wet thermometer warns when frost is likely to occur, so that your more delicate plants can be protected in the appropriate way beforehand.

Only frequent rain-gauge readings will give an accurate measurement of dryness and indicate how much water your plants need.

THE ART OF BONSAI

In ancient times, the art of bonsai was the preserve of the privileged few in China and Japan. It was associated with a highly intellectual, if not religious, approach. Some of these plants have been cultivated for several centuries, as generations of devotees of the art have lavished love and care on their plants. The transition from simple gardening to bonsai culture demands great enthusiasm. It is a difficult art, requiring a great deal of application, of which this book imparts some of the secrets.

Juniperus rigida (needle juniper) aged about 150 years.

A BRIEF HISTORY

The art of bonsai is synonymous with antiquity, since our present civilization has been unable to introduce any real innovations. The word bonsai conjures up a thousand years of art – even several thousand in some examples. It is hard to tell precisely when man first developed a passion for miniaturizing trees and growing them in trays (the word *bonsai* comes from *bon*, meaning 'tray' and *sai*, meaning tree).

Chinese before Japanese

Although it remains a controversial issue, it seems that the art of bonsai originated in China, rather than Japan, with which it is traditionally associated. One distinguished expert attributes to the Chinese originating not cultivation of single trees in trays but cultivating groups of miniature trees as part of the small decorative rock gardens, known as *pun-ching*. The art of the miniature landscape (or Japanese garden, as an ignorant European might be tempted to call it . . .) made its reappearance in the third century, in the Han dynasty to be precise. But it seems that the art of *pun-sai* or cultivating miniature trees in pots, was practised in China even before this.

Painting and literature both bear witness to the cultivation of *pun-sai* since then. However, it was in Japan that the art really took hold, particularly between the tenth and twelfth centuries under the twin influences of the Buddhist monks and the merchants, who had established trading links with China.

From *pun-sai* to *bon-sai*

Miniature trees were cultivated in pots in Japan in the ninth century (as we know from several iconographic Buddhist archives of the period), but it was not until about the thirteenth century that the art of bonsai was really absorbed into Japanese culture. For a long time, the art remained the preserve of the nobility and the priesthood, who gave it a philosophical and sacred character. Not until the beginning of the nineteenth century did the art of bonsai gain popularity at every level of society.

The World Fair in Paris in 1878 saw the first-ever presentation in Europe of bonsai collections. But they were not received with much enthusiasm, as is apparent from a report in the *Journal Hebdomadaire* by a journalist describing his visit to the Japanese pavilion: 'The outstanding plant curiosity in this garden is the miniature forest, or wooded glade, if you prefer, formed of trees that are normally immense but whose development the Japanese, like the Chinese, are skilled at limiting, so they can be grown in pots. We may not find this a particularly attractive art, but that is no reason to ignore it.'

By the time the 1889 exhibition was held eleven years later, the Japanese had realized how much the art of bonsai intrigued the French. They made it the focus of interest in their pavilion. This time, it was no longer a display of plants arranged in groups (as forests, in fact) in front of their building, but of the first ever international showing of bonsai. Although not much more enthusiastic, the reporter from the same *Journal Hebdomadaire* cast a more attentive eye over the display of bonsai: 'First of all, the sheer horticultural skill is both astounding and disconcerting. You stop short in front of these strange contorted products of cunning cultivation, so ingenious that they challenge nature, recreating it in the most minute forms, like these cedars, which are more than a century old but are not as tall as a child. Twisted by invisible storms, bent under the weight of years, the arrested foliage of these stunted plants reproduces the most capricious shapes nature is capable of in a tree's highest branches. It has taken generations of men to produce the delicate gnarling of the branches, to restrain the powerful drive of the sap, to constrain these forest giants and coax them to grow in just a few square feet. This seemingly bizarre taste, this apparently childish whim is one of the many and varied aspects of their consuming passion.' Bonsai may not have been taken up in France, but it was certainly noticed. The description given shows that these plants were true bonsai, as we understand them today. It is evident from the report that the writer had seen the basic bonsai wiring techniques and had been shown some examples a hundred or even several hundred years old.

In 1909 at the universal exhibition in London, the English gave a resounding welcome to bonsai, which struck a familiar chord with this nation of born gardeners who lovingly manicured their lawns, treating them like the family jewels. Since then, bonsai has acquired a wider audience, abandoning to some extent its traditional mystique. It was not until 1914 that the first national show was organized in Tokyo. Since then it has become an annual event.

In other parts of the world the appearance of Japanese bonsai was not followed by any great enthusiasm. This 'cunning cultivation' attracted only a few skilled devotees who delved into the secrets of those who 'challenged nature', almost always at the cost of a lengthy trip to Japan. It was not until a century after bonsai first appeared at the Paris exhibition that Europeans discovered a passion for bonsai. This love affair goes beyond a passing fancy and demands a deeper and better understanding of bonsai cultivating techniques. This is what this book is about.

First appearance of bonsai in Europe, at the 1878 World Fair in Paris.

A LITTLE PHILOSOPHY

This example of the potter's art (by J. Buccholtz) re-creates a Tibetan monastery: a fine example of the philosophical aspect of bonsai culture.

Whereas growing bonsai in the West is regarded as a pleasant leisure pursuit producing some really original plants for display in the house, on the balcony or in the garden, the Oriental, particularly the Japanese, gains far deeper intellectual satisfaction from their creation.

It seems that bonsai were not originally produced as they are today, from seed, grafting or layering. A uniquely shaped plant would first have to be found in the mountains or forests. The search for such a plant was endowed with the symbolic meaning of a 'quest for the inner self' and a return to the origins of man. It is in the ceaseless effort involved in such a search for perfection, for a flawless subject hidden among the giants, that such beauty may eventually be discovered.

The art of bonsai can only be achieved in harmony with nature, coupled with the desire to dominate it and to repro-duce faithfully, though on a different scale, what nature creates.

To a certain extent, it is questionable whether the art of bonsai can be considered gardening in the true sense. The techniques are very different. In conventional gardening the gardener strives to subdue nature to produce the plants he wants, not those that develop spontaneously. Where the conventional gardener will cut a hedge or shape and train a fruit tree, the bonsai enthusiast is at pains to preserve the natural shapes of his trees. It is a search for true perfection, reflecting the harmony between man and nature, the universal ideal. This is one of the fundamental precepts of oriental culture, in which the shaping of destiny is an integral concept. The art of bonsai is a practical exercise that allows empathy with nature and a respect for its natural shapes, while showing that one is master over it.

It is worth recalling that the art of bonsai originated with Buddhist monks in China, who gave the growing of trees in trays an almost religious significance. For them it was a way of establishing a special link between God, creator of the universe and nature in all its forms, including mankind, striving to follow the divine path by controlling the process of growth and form in trees, though on a human scale. The nobility wanted to take part in growing bonsai at certain periods, having no intention of leaving this privilege to the priests alone. To cultivate bonsai is, to a certain extent, to show an understanding of the concept of the creation of the world: perhaps in a way to participate in creation at the everyday level. Looked at in this light, the sustained effort demanded by the cultivation of bonsai cannot be regarded as arduous or pedantic, as many an uninitiated European might at first think!

STYLES AND TRADITIONS

A large part of the art of bonsai consists of imitating nature, by shaping the trees grown in trays to look like those found in the countryside or forest. This is why the most widely used shapes have been given names, which make up an official catalogue of some of the characteristic forms from which the bonsai enthusiast can choose. The tree must conform to the type chosen, the whole art consisting of cutting, pruning and wiring the plant to the chosen shape. These 'official' shapes, the formation of which will be described, all originate from Japan.

To obtain these characteristic shapes requires a degree of skill, adaptable material, and above all, a great deal of patience. For a tree, unlike a man, has eternity before it – particularly when it benefits from careful tending.

A magnificent example of the informal upright shape (*moyôgi*) created in a 200-year-old pine.

Single trees

The following are single trees with one trunk grown in containers.

CHOKKAN: this is an upright tree, which has a vertical trunk and progressively smaller branches. The branches are arranged symmetrically, forming the pyramidal shape which is characteristic of the giant conifers.

MOYÔGI: an almost upright tree, with spiral development of the trunk, which decreases towards the crown.

SHAKAN: a tree whose single trunk leans sharply to the right or left. Its branches are fairly uniformly arranged, and are positioned on opposite sides of the trunk.

BAN KAN: a tree whose trunk is curved and twisted and even, in some cases, really knotted.

HAN-KENGAÏ: a 'semi-cascading' form, characteristic of plants whose branches grow out of one side of the trunk, while not really weeping. This shape is frequently associated with the *Shakan* style.

KENGAÏ: a cascading tree, with a strongly bent trunk, whose branches hang right over the container.

FUKINAGASHI: a form also described as 'windblown'. The trunk leans to a greater or lesser extent and the branches all face the same direction (the same way the trunk leans), as if battered by the wind.

HÔKIDACHI: an upright tree, whose branches begin to sprout out at a certain height, giving it its characteristic, broom-like appearance. The elm is particularly suited to this very symmetrical shape.

BUNJINGI: a 'literati' form of tree, imitating calligraphy. An elegant form with a slightly slanting trunk, whose branches and foliage develop only at the crown.

ISHITZUKI: a very specific form for plants grown on or in the crevices of rock-like stones or boulders. A 'rock-dweller', this is a very effective form, some plants developing a spectacular arrangement of knotty aerial roots.

Chokkan

Moyôgi

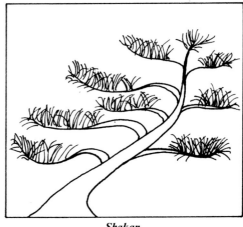

Shakan

Han-Kengaï

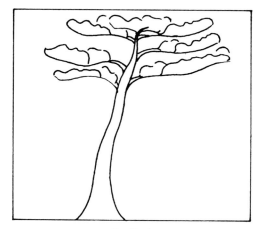

Bunjingi

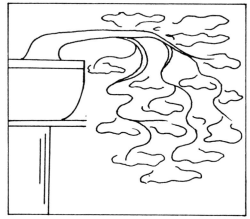

Kengaï

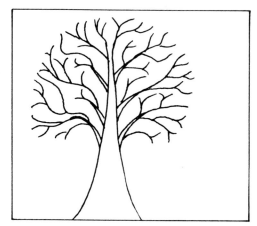

Hôkidachi

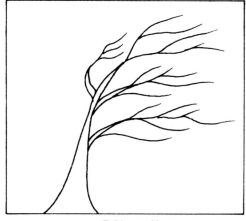

Fukinagashi

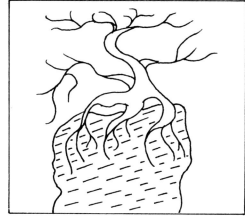

Ishitsuki

Neagari
(roots visible)

Nejikan
(twisted trunk)

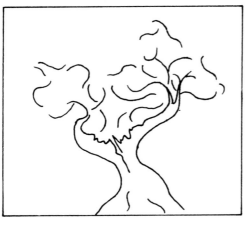

Sabamiki
(cleft trunk)

Sankan

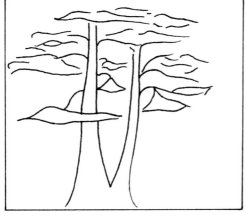

Sokan

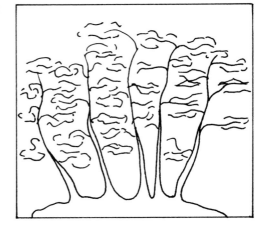

Ikadabuki

Kadushi

Juniperus chinensis **in a perfect** *Sankan* **form, with three trunks clearly visible.**

Netsuranari

Korabuki
(turtle back)

Trees with several trunks

These are literally trees which have several trunks growing from a single root. The following are examples.

SOKAN: the simplest form, a double trunk growing from a forked base.
SANKAN: not two, but three trunks growing out of one stock.

In these two cases, the size of the trunks growing out of the base should not be identical. In the *Sokan* style one of the trunks is thicker than the other: this is the 'father', the other trunk being the 'son'. In the *Sankan* style two trunks are larger than the other, and these are the 'mother' and 'father', with the smaller trunk the 'son'.

KADUSHI: a series of trunks with multiple branches growing from a single root, branched like the types described above, but usually with an odd number of trunks.
IKADA BUKI: a variation of the above known as 'raft' bonsai, but with the trunk lying just below the surface of the soil and the branches, which rise vertically, giving the illusion of a group of trees planted side by side.
NETSURANARI: this is a spreading, 'rambling' shape, obtained by growing various trunks from a single, connected root base lying on the surface of the soil, again giving the impression of several trees planted side by side.

A forest of *Serissa japonica*. The display is enhanced by some rocks in the tray.

A forest of maples (*Acer buergeranum = A. trifidum*): arranged on a flat tray (*Yose Ue* style).

Groups of trees or forests

The desire to imitate nature provides the incentive for planting several trees in a container, to form groups of trees that recall a forest.

This effect results from planting several trees of the same species or variety, though often of differing ages and subsequently differing sizes. The way they are arranged can suggest a simple glade or a veritable forest. In the latter case, different trees may be used, with various combinations of evergreens to provide contrast.

The *Yose Ue* style (two or more trees in one container), uses a flat tray, or flat, moss-covered stone base. The trees making up a forest may, themselves, be different styles of the single or multiple trunk tree just described.

The most popular single trunk shapes to create this effect are the *Hokidachi, Fukinagashi, Bunjinki* and *Ishitsuki* bonsai, as well as some multiple trunk forms.

These forests, always spectacular even when the trees are young, are extremely popular today. It should be said that they require special, sometimes very exacting care. Do not imagine that a forest will hide the imperfection of a single tree. . . .

Particular attention should be paid to watering during warm weather, since a number of trees sharing the same container will need a considerable amount.

Profile of a deciduous forest.

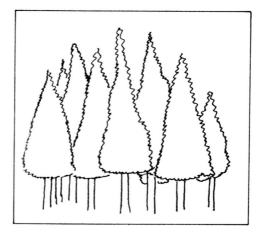

Profile of a coniferous forest.

Forest of *Chamaecyparis obtusa*. The trees are arranged in perfect harmony.

This group of Virginian sumachs was originally dug up from the wild.

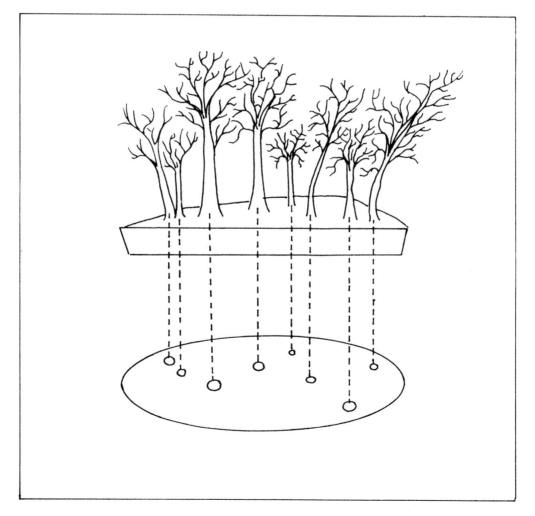

Planting plan designed to produce a miniature forest (*Yose Ue*).

OBTAINING YOUR BONSAI

Although the ancient philosophical traditions of the Far East required you to find your own bonsai in nature (a quest for self), it is certainly much simpler (and more efficient) these days to acquire your bonsai from a professional grower or importer of established trees. However, it is also possible for the most patient among us to produce our own bonsai, either from seed, cuttings, layering or grafting. A number of grafting techniques are described, step by step, over the next few pages.

COLLECTING

We have seen that collecting – finding bonsai in nature – featured strongly in the philosophy of this highly intellectual exercise. To the Buddhist monk or Samurai it was inconceivable that bonsai could be created in the same way as a common vegetable. Crucial to the philosophy was a return to nature, a symbolic quest for 'self'.

In Japanese, the quest for a tree in its natural surroundings is called *Yamadori* and bonsai obtained in this way are *Yamadori Shitate*. This has the advantage of allowing you to choose the shape you want, as well as a tree which is already several years, or even decades, old. Conversely, it is rare to find a tree which conforms to the established styles. It is often harder to correct the defects inherent in an established tree than to shape a young tree produced from seed, cuttings or layering. But the satisfaction of finding a superb tree, even if it does not conform to the established styles, can be profound.

Before describing the methods of collecting, it is as well to define the limitations of this practice.

Dense undergrowth of this type provides perfect cover for young trees suitable for training as bonsai.

Legal restrictions

The scope for collecting from nature is, in fact, very limited. Removing plants from land owned by the state is strictly prohibited. There are, justifiably, severe penalties for removing any type of plant from forests which are set in protected natural parkland.

Where land is privately owned, you should always, of course, ask the owner's permission to dig up plants. Even then, plants can only be lifted if the land is not set in protected parkland, and the plant itself is not protected by law. Clearly the legal restrictions are numerous, severely limiting the possibility of collecting many trees from the wild.

Conifers reproduce easily in the wild. Suitable seedlings could well be collected from the undergrowth beneath pines.

Where to look

Even if there is no legal restriction to collecting, the location still needs to be suitable for producing potential bonsai subjects.

Stunted growth in trees can only result from conditions unfavourable to normal development. This could be caused by the area's climate (high altitude, for example), poor light (such as dense undergrowth or permanent shade from a cliff), or even poor soil (in sandy moorland or stony ground, perhaps).

When to lift

In principle, all transplanting should be carried out during the plant's dormant period before the year's growth commences. The considerable climatic variations in areas where there is a good chance of finding suitable bonsai material make it difficult to pinpoint the correct months for transplanting. But as a rule of thumb, deciduous trees should be transplanted in autumn and conifers in early spring (through to mid-spring in temperate zones). In either case, plants should not be lifted while frost persists: the ideal time is after rain, when the earth is well soaked.

How to lift

The roots of a tree form a complex network often searching far into the earth for the water and nutrients it needs. To give the lifted tree the best chance to become established, roots and rootlets should suffer as little damage as possible. The plant should never be wrenched up: take the utmost care to dig a trench deep enough to ensure that all the roots can be lifted, with as much of the surrounding earth as possible. Also take some soil from around the tree to ease the transition from nature to tray. It is more important to lift deciduous trees with as much of the surrounding soil as possible, than it is for conifers, which can be transplanted with almost bare roots and still have a chance of establishment.

Before transplanting a tree collected from the wild, its roots should be trimmed.

How to move

The essential function of roots is to allow the tree to 'drink' and this is why it is vital to keep them moist during transport. The most natural way is to take a little moss, moisten it and wrap it around the roots. If you cannot find any moss, use cotton wool. The wrapped root ball should then be covered in plastic or aluminium foil. If transport is to take several days, the rootball must be moistened again. For trees with only a few fine roots, and especially outside the dormant season, spray the tree with a transplanting spray. This should be allowed to dry before the tree is lifted. Before wrapping, the roots should also be sprayed. This spray acts as a sealant and helps to stop the tree losing moisture by transpiration, thus giving it a greater chance of surviving the shock of transplanting. Some recommend trimming the roots and foliage before transport, just after lifting. This consists of pruning some of the leaves and the ends of the roots to limit evaporation through the leaves and to make absorbing water at root level easier. It also provides an opportunity to re-establish the balance between the branches and roots.

Cut only a little foliage from a tree which has many roots and cut only a few roots from a tree which has sparse branches and leaves.

GROWING FROM SEED

Growing from seed remains the simplest and most natural method of propagation but by no means the most reliable. It also requires a great deal of patience, particularly with very slow-growing trees. It can take anything up to five years to obtain a bonsai from seed.

How to obtain seeds

Look for wild seeds in autumn. With a little skill, you will find a variety of seeds lying about. But you may encounter the dual problem of finding which tree the seed has come from and what kind it is. This is no problem with acorns or chestnuts, but the problem becomes acute where several species of conifer grow in the same place.

It should also be emphasized that the chances of successfully germinating seeds found in nature are very poor. Some seeds, for example, may have been attacked by parasites which threaten germination or the plant's successful development, while others may well have been contaminated by viral or fungal disease.

But do not let this discourage you from collecting a suitable specimen from the forest and experiencing the joy of growing a tree from seed you have found yourself. You should just be aware of the risks and limitations. One reliable solution is to buy selected commercial seeds. These offer a high success rate for germination and the fact that they are sold commercially means there is less risk of diseases and parasites. Seeds sold commercially expressly for producing bonsai come mainly from the Far East and are of species particularly well-suited to this method of growing. But no seeds, having germinated, grow into dwarf trees without special care. The miniaturizing technique entails no genetic modification of the trees. So bonsai seeds will produce

The seeds of this superb variegated holly could soon be ready for collection and sowing, but the results are uncertain.

Unlike seeds collected from the wild, commercially sold seeds have a good chance of germinating (these are varieties for bonsai).

Packet of selected seeds and container filled with sand, ready for stratification.

Spread the seeds over the moist sand covering the base of the container.

After spreading the seeds over the sand, cover them with wet sand and . . . wait. Seeds may be ready to sow in the spring.

normal sized progeny if not specially treated to produce bonsai, just as seeds intended to produce normal trees can also form bonsai. A word about the magnificent trees often pictured on seed packets. These are superb examples of what can be achieved but not the kind of result you can rely upon if you buy the packet. Many enthusiasts who have not been forewarned have been disappointed by not producing as fine a specimen as the one shown on the packet or in the catalogue.

Preparing the seeds

Whereas many of the smaller seeds can be sown directly in autumn or spring, this is not the case for the larger seeds, particularly if they have a hard coating like a shell. This is true of most tree seeds. They should be left to soak in tepid water for at least 24 hours. If the protective coating is hard or thick, it may be necessary to make an incision, without damaging the seed inside. If the seed is protected by an outer shell, this should be carefully broken open with pliers, taking care not to crush the seed.

Often the seed will not germinate without special treatment, known as stratification. This technique consists of forming alternate layers of seeds and moist sand. This softens the seeds and helps them to germinate, which considerably increases the chances of success. Be prepared to wait, as this form of seed preparation may take several months or a year, depending on the species.

Before sowing, it is worth soaking the seeds in disinfectant to limit the risk of fungal diseases when the seedlings start to sprout (e.g. damping off disease of seedlings). However, as damping off is one of the most likely causes of failure with seedlings, you should be prepared to spray or dust with a fungicide within a few days of the seeds germinating.

If you are using bought seeds, check the packet to make sure that the seeds are not out of date as failure will be higher than normal.

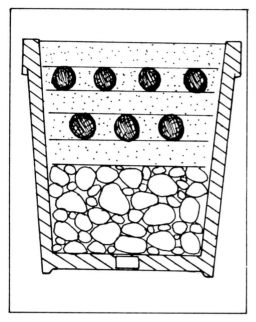

Stratifying tree seeds.

A sieve is essential for creating a fine-textured soil mixture for seed-sowing.

Where to sow

SOIL

For most trees, the ideal compost for seed-sowing consists of equal parts of peat, loam and sand. This standard composition can be adjusted to suit the special demands of particular species. Although this mixture suits most plants, it cannot be used for heathland shrubs, which need a very acid soil.

The best for these seedlings is pure peat, or peat with sand. Take particular care to ensure that the potting compost is kept moist. So as not to impede the development of young roots, the potting compost should be cleared of the larger impurities and any pebbles which it may contain. It may even be useful to pass it through a coarse garden sieve. Any soil used to cover the seeds should be passed through a fine mesh garden sieve. To prevent disease, the soil should be disinfected with a product based on formalin or with steam. This could produce good results with earth taken from nature, which should be carefully passed through a sieve. Any unwanted seeds and fragments of root should be re-

Filling a traditional clay pot with sieved compost mixture.

moved to prevent them growing at the same time as the tree seeds sown. Such 'weeds' are difficult to remove later without damaging the seedling.

CONTAINERS

Once the seedling has sprouted its first pair of leaves, it should be potted on several times. Great care should be taken not to damage the seedling or its roots. The roots are especially delicate and should not be pruned at this stage. Therefore the container used for sowing can be considered temporary and not as important as the tray in which the bonsai will later be planted.

The stratified seeds are scattered over the compost mixture as they are here.

If the seeds (here ginkgo) are protected by a shell, this should be cracked with pliers.

The depth of compost that covers the seeds depends on the size of the seeds.

After breaking the shell, remove the seed from its protective covering.

If, as here, the seeds are quite large, the surface soil should be firmed. Here, a traditional trowel is being used to do this.

Having been removed from their shells, the seeds can be sown. As germination has been made easier, stratification is unnecessary.

Though some may favour sowing seeds in trays or bowls, we recommend small pots, especially for big seeds. A peat pot has the advantage of avoiding the shock of transplanting, since the pot itself disintegrates. But watch that the peat does not dry out. By contrast, clay pots hold the moisture in the compost very well indeed.

Sowing technique

Whatever container is used, it is essential to cover the base with a layer of fine gravel or sand to ensure good drainage after watering. The container should have a drainage hole, so excess water can drain away.

Fill the pot with suitable potting compost to within about 2 cm ($\frac{3}{4}$ in) of the rim. Lightly pat down the soil with a small wooden presser. Sow the seeds thinly so they are not overcrowded when they germinate. Large seeds can be sown individually, smaller seeds sown with a seeder. If you do not have a seeder, use a piece of stiff cardboard folded in two from which the seeds are gently tapped.

Now cover the seeds with a layer of compost passed through a fine sieve. The depth of compost covering the seeds will vary with the size of the seeds. The largest will need 1–2 cm ($\frac{3}{8}$–$\frac{3}{4}$ in) layer of compost, whereas smaller seeds require only a mere dusting. The tiniest seeds are best not covered, as this can stop them sprouting.

The surface of the compost should be lightly firmed with a wooden tamp or presser: do not firm it too much, as the seeds should still be able to 'breathe'. Immediately afterwards, give them their first careful watering. Give them a fine spray, so the surface layer of soil is not disturbed. Again, the size of the seeds and thickness of the surface layer will influence the method of watering. Large, well covered seeds can be watered with a can fitted with a fine rose, but small seeds covered with a thin layer of compost should be watered with a fine mist from a hand sprayer. Tiny seeds not covered

A disk of paper is here being placed over the top of the pot of newly-sown seeds.

The disk prevents the surface compost being disturbed during watering.

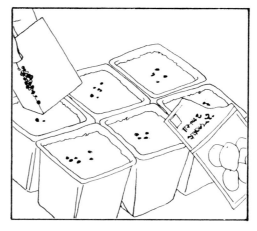

Sow the smallest seeds from a piece of folded paper or thin cardboard as they may stick to your hand. Then cover them with a dusting of soil.

Peat pots are excellent for seed sowing.

Before sowing or potting up, soak peat pots.

This young maple was sown in its plastic pot.

The moist peat pots can now be filled with compost.

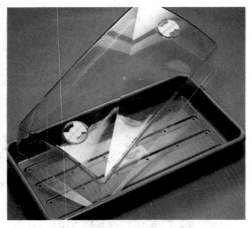

This mini-propagator makes an excellent container for pots of sown seeds or potted bonsai seedlings.

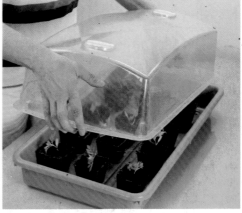

After sowing or potting, replace the plastic cover of the propagator.

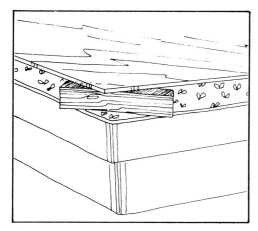

A wedge will raise the sheet of glass enough to permit air to circulate and prevent condensation.

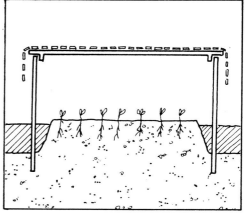

Seedlings planted out in a nursery must be protected from direct sun.

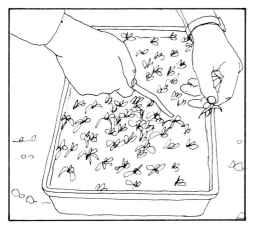

When seedlings sown in trays have developed, they must be planted out.

with compost should be watered from below by standing the container in a tray containing water until the compost is saturated. Be careful that the water which rises by capillary action does not disperse the seeds when it reaches the surface.

A propagator is an ideal container: keep the pots in it in a shady place at a temperature of 15–20°C (60–70°F). Trays and bowls should be covered with a sheet of glass, leaving one corner open to let the air circulate, to limit evaporation and to keep the soil surface at the right temperature. If you do not have a sheet of glass, stand the containers in a frame or, if the temperature is likely to

remain above 10°C (50°F) and there is no night frost, simply stand on a balcony. There is normally a risk of frost in temperate zones from late autumn, and so seeds should then be taken in and stood in a cool place near a sunny window. Make sure that watering is frequent enough if the room temperature is warm and the atmosphere dry. It may be necessary to stand the container in water regularly once the seeds have sprouted.

Once you have sown your seeds, you will need a great deal of patience, since most tree seeds take several months to germinate. Some may not even sprout until the following year!

In every case, regular watering and a constant temperature will increase your chances of success. Even before its birth, the embryonic bonsai demands complete devotion!

Initial care
Germination is followed by the rapid development of the young plant which quickly develops roots, loses its seed-leaves and produces true leaves. But the seedling remains fragile and so a watchful eye should be kept on it. Make sure the moisture level is adequate to keep the plant growing but not excessive, so it encourages fungal disease, such as

Professional nurserymen raise their plants (conifers here) in polythene tunnels or greenhouses.

A small metal-framed greenhouse built from a kit, suitable for amateur use.

damping off. To avoid severe dehydration, the seedling should not be exposed to direct sunlight. It should be gradually hardened to both cold and heat. If the season is suitable, the seedling can be potted on after a few months. At this stage, an ordinary clay pot should be used, as the plant cannot yet be thought of as a bonsai. One can now start to feed the plant with fertilizer to promote its development. The pot should be stood outdoors, weather permitting.

If you have a garden, you might be able to plant your tree in a bed for its first year, although you will have to monitor development carefully, to ensure that the seedling does not grow too quickly to be suitable for bonsai training later. These roots sometimes reach astonishing proportions, to stunning effect. Such bonsai can make a spectacular contribution to the decor of a room.

Bonsai treatment should start in the second year after germination, though its first potting in a bonsai tray will not take place until the end of its third year. Throughout this time, whether you use pots or plant out in beds, make sure that no weeds develop to the detriment of the seedling.

In hot weather, break the crust of soil that forms around the base of the young plant to prevent too much evaporation by capillary action.

Professional growers offer a selection of potential bonsai which have already matured for those who choose not to produce their own.

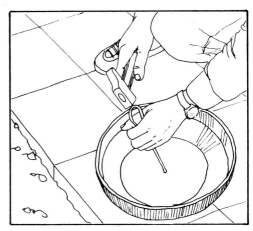

Before transplanting into a special bonsai container, use an ordinary pot after providing it with a drainage hole.

VEGETATIVE PROPAGATION

This term is used to describe all the techniques by which plants are grown other than from seed. This means producing roots from growing branches.

This category also includes grafting, although here two plants are linked rather than root growth being produced.

Cuttings

Without doubt, this is the simplest and speediest method of propagation. It is also a method with the best chance of obtaining a plant similar to the parent plant, which is not so likely from seeds.

Roots have to be produced by a living twig cut from a tree, so it can pursue an independent existence. In principle, given the right conditions, it should be possible to take cuttings from any plant.

Direct contact with water should cause the cutting to grow roots; this can be easily proved by putting a twig in a glass of water, although this method usually only succeeds with plants with good rooting properties, like succulents. Woody twigs require special conditions if they are to make lasting roots.

All the materials necessary for taking cuttings: soil sand, pots, hormone rooting powder and, of course, fresh cuttings.

TAKING CUTTINGS

Use a sharp blade (such as a budding knife) or good secateurs, to make a clean cut. Disinfect the blade with alcohol or formalin or by sterilizing with a flame to prevent the spread of infection.

The simplest method is to cut a twig about 15 cm (6 in) long. Trim the base of the cutting diagonally (simple cutting) and remove its lower leaves. You can also cut a section of the parent branch with the twig (T-shape cutting) or keep some of the bark of the branch (heel cutting). The latter method has the advantage of exposing more of the

The compost mixture used for rooting cuttings consists of peat and sand. Mix it well so it has a uniform colour.

Thoroughly moisten the compost before planting your cuttings.

Taking a cutting from a *Chamaecyparis lawsoniana* 'Aureovariegata' with secateurs.

Cedars lend themselves perfectly to bonsai. Here, a cutting is taken from a Mount Atlas cedar (*Cedrus atlantica* var. *glauca*).

cambium cells, enhancing root growth and the chances of survival.

Where shoots have leaves, keep some of the leaf nodes at the base. When inserted in the compost, roots tend to grow from these nodes. In fact, some plant cuttings, such as those from vines, only grow if the nodes or buds are buried.

When should cuttings be taken? This simple question is the subject of much controversy. Without wanting to evade the issue, one could say that cuttings can be taken throughout the year, though the best times vary from species to species, since the growing cycle of each plant is significantly different.

Although cuttings can be taken from some species from spring onwards, the best results are generally obtained using the year's new growth, if woody enough, which usually means that the twigs will not be ready for cutting until the summer. This way, the cutting will not have to suffer the shock of major growth in the weeks immediately after rooting. Since the first growth does not begin until the autumn, it does not proceed in

To help rooting, cuttings can be planted in bundles, buried to a third of their length against the foot of a wall, which will protect them during winter.

earnest until the next spring, by which time the plant is much stronger.

Cutting techniques

Although basically simple, taking cuttings demands great care. This is the price of achieving a high success rate.

CONTAINER AND CONTENTS: Use plastic, clay or, even better, peat pots. Potting compost should be light: peat mixed with sand is ideal.

PREPARING CUTTINGS: If leafy, keep only the upper leaves. Cut off a portion of the remaining leaves to limit transpiration and subsequent dehydration of the cutting. Remove the lower leaves, but take care to retain the buds in their axils. Dip the bases of the cuttings in hormone powder, then gently shake off excess.

PLANTING THE CUTTING: Give the contents of the pot a good watering: the best way is to stand the pot in water. Make a hole in the compost for the cutting with a stick or pencil. If you insert the cutting without making a hole, the rooting hormone will be left on the

Cuttings should not be longer than about 10 cm (4 in). Here, a *Ficus benjamina* cutting.

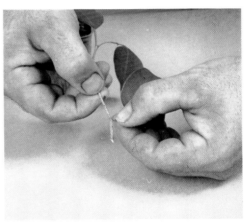

Any leaves at the base of the cutting (which would be buried) should be removed.

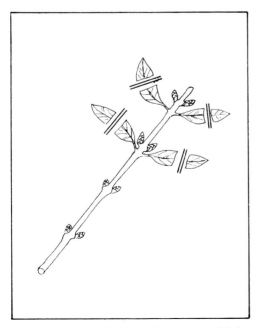

To reduce evaporation from the leaves and help prevent dehydration of the cutting, clip away about half the leaf blade.

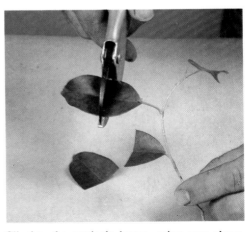

Clipping the cutting's leaves, using very sharp secateurs. If you use a blunt pair you will probably damage the tissues.

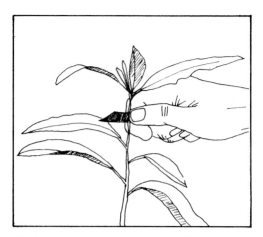

Cuttings can be taken with a budding knife, or similar sharp bladed knife.

The 'eye' or bud in the axil of the leaf stalk indicates where the cutting should be taken.

surface. Firm the compost gently around the stem base with your fingers, so the cutting fits snugly in the compost. Water generously.

Dehydration is the main cause of failure in cuttings. Professionals put their cuttings under a mist spray. The amateur is limited to watering his cuttings at least twice a day while they are growing. A good way to limit transpiration is to place a translucent plastic cover over the cuttings, at least while they are rooting. But watch carefully for any signs of mould.

The appearance of new shoots usually indicates rooting and is a sign that the cutting has taken. But some plants can survive on their own food reserves and may develop shoots without having produced roots. This is why you must be very patient and wait until you are absolutely sure that the cutting has taken before potting it on.

ADVANTAGES OF CUTTINGS

The main advantage without doubt is the exact reproduction of the features of the parent plant, an advantage shared by other vegetative methods of propagation, particularly layering, which is described later.

In terms of bonsai creation, cuttings have the advantage of a specimen plant on which the desired bonsai can be

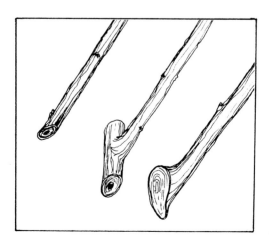

Three ways of taking a cutting: (left to right) simple, T-shape and with a heel. The third is popular.

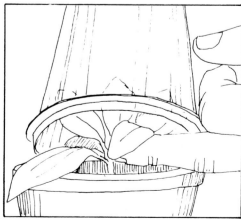

Some cuttings can be kept covered for several days to limit transpiration.

modelled. In other words, you can choose exactly which style or shape you want and duplicate what you see – a considerable time saving when producing bonsai.

Another considerable advantage is that once the cutting has taken you will have a plant that is much more advanced than a seed that has just germinated.

Although your cutting might be growing strongly, remember that it will take a number of weeks for the root ball to establish itself. So treat the new tree with care. Pruning can be started as soon as necessary, and as well as starting to form the shape of the tree it also helps to stop the new roots from overworking.

Some cuttings are no more than a well-developed leaf bud.

1. Preparing a cedar cutting. The needles at the base are removed.

3. Make a small hole in the compost and insert the cutting.

2. Dip the cutting in hormone rooting powder. The chances of rooting are then greatly improved.

4. Firm the compost round the base of the cutting. Water well and firm again.

Layering

This technique is similar to taking cuttings to the extent that it is based on the principle of producing spontaneous root growth from a shoot. But in layering, rooting takes place without the cutting being separated from its parent. Roots develop after a part of a branch is buried in the soil or in other medium conditions that favour rooting. This is a gentler method of propagation, since the cutting is not severed from its parent until it is well rooted.

There are many different methods of layering and we shall describe only the most familiar. A broad distinction can be made between ground layering, where a branch or shoot is bent down to the ground, and air layering.

GROUND LAYERING

Here roots grow where a branch or shoot is in direct contact with the earth. This type of propagation is considered spontaneous, insofar as it is often found in nature on plants with trailing branches, such as wild rhododendrons.

SIMPLE GROUND LAYERING: This technique is most like the natural phenomenon. A low branch is bent down to the ground, where it is held in place by a wire hoop. The part of the branch touching the ground is lightly covered with earth, the rest being supported by a stake. To stimulate rooting, the buried part should be brushed with hormone rooting powder and its bark lightly scored.

Simple layering is usually carried out during the dormant period, so roots should appear in spring. The layer can be severed from its parent in autumn, but, to be quite sure, it can always be left till the end of the following winter.

To root a layer in a pot, just bend the parent branch into a pot, then proceed exactly as above. As some branches might not be inclined to sit in the pot in the way you would like them to, particular care should be taken to secure the potential layering to stop it 'springing' from the pot.

1. The part of the layer to be buried in the ground should be stripped of its leaves.

2. The defoliated part should be dipped in hormone rooting powder.

3. Bury the part of branch you wish to layer and hold it in place with a ring or metal hoop.

4. Tread the ground firmly to ensure the branch is in close contact with the soil.

7. In just a few months this branch, buried in the ground, had produced roots.

5. The part that one wants to form roots should be well watered.

8. To make transplanting easier it might be more helpful to layer the branch in a pot.

6. The layer should not be severed until well rooted. Use secateurs and cut close to the ground.

9. Water regularly, as the plant cannot obtain moisture naturally by capillary action.

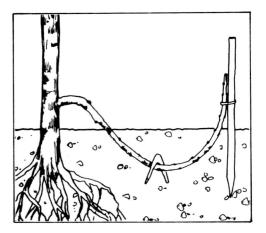

Simple layering: note the stake supporting the plant being produced by layering.

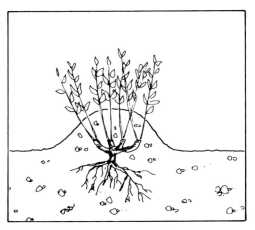

Stooling: a number of new plants develop above the root stock.

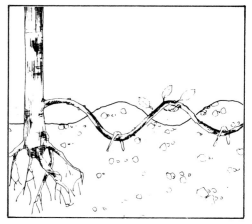

Serpentine layering: make as many arches as you like, if the branch is supple enough. Separate as in simple layering.

STOOLING: This is only possible with shrubs which tolerate heavy pruning. This method involves drastic pruning, cutting the bush right down to its crown before the new season's growth starts. Then mound or cover the base of the plant with soil and in spring, when the shoots develop, the roots will have started to form at their base, above the crown. The mound can be cleared and the layers exposed and planted out during the course of the following winter. Root development can be noted at this stage and if it is inadequate, the layers should be left attached to their parent for a further year.

CHINESE LAYERING: In this method, the branch is stripped of its leaves, leaving all the eyes (leaf buds) intact and laid along the ground and covered with earth. The leaf buds will then develop vertical shoots, which sprout from the ground to form rooted layers. To separate them, just cut the parent branch between the shoots. This should be done during the winter after the shoots sprout.

SERPENTINE LAYERING: This is a variation of the simple layering method. Instead of being buried once, the branch is arched and staked several times, forming a succession of undulations. Otherwise, this method is exactly as for simple layering with the lower parts pegged in contact with the soil and scored and dipped in hormone rooting powder. Severing the cuttings is again as for simple layering.

Of the methods described, simple layering is recommended as the best way of producing a bonsai, since it allows you to choose the style you want. It is possible to select a particular branch for its shape. Make sure that the aerial part of the layer is well supported, otherwise it could become deformed while the roots are forming.

Where simple layering takes place in a pot, a method which avoids the shock of transplanting, the cutting should be regularly watered before and after it is separated from its parent.

Air layering

This is a completely artificial way of propagating, which offers a number of advantages for bonsai creation. Well-formed plants can be obtained quickly but, most important, the girth of its trunk is that of a much older established tree. The technique is relatively simple, though the results cannot be guaranteed. Be warned that a branch prepared for air layering is irretrievably damaged, if the operation is not a success.

As with simple layering, this method will allow you to choose which part of the branch you use. Its shape should suit the style of bonsai you wish to grow. Unlike simple layering, air layering allows you to use part of a branch from any level of the plant.

You will need a very sharp grafting knife, a polythene sheet, a piece of string or raffia or two elastic bands, and some moss cut from the base of a tree, perhaps. Select the part of the branch that will form the base of the bonsai, make two cuts right round the branch, 2–3 cm ($\frac{3}{4}$–$1\frac{1}{4}$ in) apart, taking care not to damage the wood. Carefully remove the bark between the two incisions and sprinkle some hormone rooting powder on the exposed part with tweezers. Then cover with damp moss and form a sleeve from the polythene to keep the moss in place. Tie to keep the sleeve tightly sealed at both ends. Roots will grow into the moss. This takes about one to two months for deciduous trees but three to six months for conifers, which are more difficult to produce by air layering. The incision can be ringed with copper wire which is inserted in the cut to slow down sap circulation, causing the tree to grow new roots in an effort to survive. Air layering is usually most successful in spring, at a time of most active growth, when the leaves first appear. Obviously, the layer should not be severed from its parent until its roots are well developed. The roots will usually grow through the polythene sheet on their own. The branch can then be cut below the incision, taking care not to damage the roots. Roots grown by this method are particularly delicate and although they will be tightly wrapped around the new tree, you should not attempt to unravel them. Once the tree is planted they will unravel themselves naturally. Separation and planting should only be carried out during dormancy. Air layering is also useful for shortening the trunk of a bonsai which has grown too tall.

This method of propagation is particularly suitable for indoor plants and for those raised in a greenhouse, since it is easier to keep the moss in which the roots grow damp in the controlled environment of a greenhouse.

In air layering, a ring is cut in the branch chosen.

The incision is treated with hormone rooting powder and wrapped in damp moss. It is then enclosed in polythene.

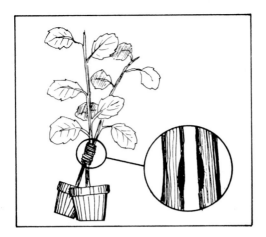

1. **Approach grafting: a sliver of bark is cut from stock and scion and the two are placed alongside and tied together.**

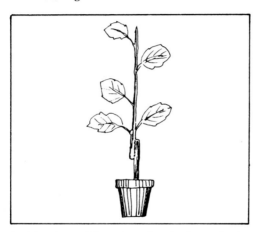

2. **After the graft has taken: the scion is growing in exactly the same line as the stock.**

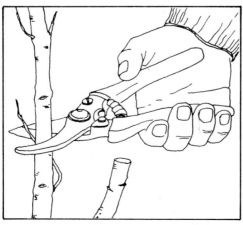

Cleft and crown grafts require a clean, horizontal cut in the parent stock. Trim the newly-made cut with a pruning knife.

Grafting

This method of propagation is based on joining the living tissue of two growing plants, which may be different, yet closely related, compatible species. The method allies the aerial part, or scion, to the stock growing in the ground. The plant produced will have the characteristics of the scion.

Grafting is of interest for creating bonsai, since it guarantees the transmission of very specific characteristics, which is not certain from seeds. Above all it is a way of obtaining a particular shape and style quickly. Some plants can only be obtained in this way, such as certain fruit trees from stones or pips, which make most attractive bonsai.

DIFFERENT GRAFTING METHODS
A great many grafting methods are used to unite various plants, most of them requiring little but highly specialized equipment: a double bladed grafting knife with one straight and one curved blade, raffia (for grafts which need tying) and special mastic for grafts which do not need tying.

The various methods described will unite one plant to another efficiently, but remember that grafting often leaves a visible scar, which can spoil the appearance of a bonsai.

APPROACH GRAFTING: This is the 'gentlest' method, since the scion is not removed from its parent until the graft has taken. The technique is simple: remove a piece of bark from both scion and stock with a grafting knife (taking care not to damage the wood). Then press the two against each other so the cambium layers are in contact and tie with raffia. Do not use mastic. If the rings of growing tissue coincide perfectly, the two plants will quickly fuse. Bring the two plants together when their growth is most active, preferably in early spring. When the graft has taken, the plants can be separated, but not before the end of the following winter. Then cut the stock above the join, and cut the scion just below the join. The binding can now be removed. To help heal the scar and to make it less unsightly, cover the wounds with mastic.

CLEFT GRAFTING: Here, the parent stock is cut through horizontally. The cut should be made with sharp secateurs or a saw and should be perfectly clean. Trim the cut with the curved blade of a grafting knife, which should also be used to make a vertical slit in the centre of the parent stock. Trim the base of the scion with the curved knife blade until its wedge shape slides easily into the slit. Then tie the graft and, lastly, seal it with mastic.

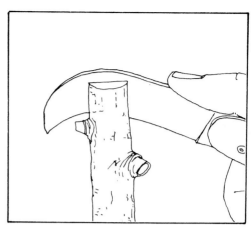

The stock is cut through horizontally. The blade of a grafting knife is used to make a vertical slit.

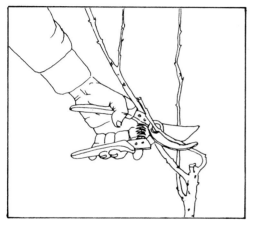

Scion material is initially cut with secateurs although only the tip of the shoot is used for grafting.

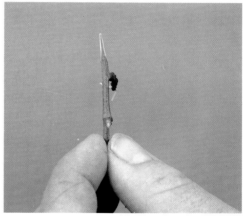

2. With a grafting knife, trim the base of the scion to a wedge shape.

1. Prepare the stock for a cleft graft by making a vertical slit. The blade of the grafting knife should first be sterilized in a flame.

3. Carefully fit the scion into the cleft so that the cut tissue is in close contact with the cut tissue of the stock.

4. Having inserted the graft, bind it firmly in place with raffia.

5. If you have no raffia, use twine but do not pull it too tight.

6. Use mastic to bond graft. You can apply it with a wooden stick.

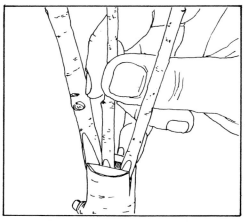

It is possible to insert two or three scions in the same slit in the stock.

7. Cover all the raffia and the cut in the stock with mastic, to help the healing process.

1. To prepare a crown graft start by making three vertical incisions through the bark but without damaging the wood of the stock.

CROWN GRAFTING: Like cleft grafting, this needs a good, clean cut, but the slits should not be made right across the stem. Vertical slits should be made in the bark in three places, 3–4 cm (1¼–1½ in) apart. Cut the ends of the scions to a taper, then insert in the slits. A grafting knife is essential for making the slits and lightly peeling back the bark, as well as for trimming the scion. Use the small spatula at the other end of the knife to peel back the bark. When the scions are in place, bind the graft and apply mastic. This type of graft will be of special interest to those wishing to produce 'broom' or 'weeping' style bonsai.

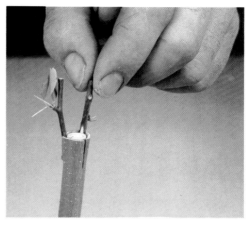

4. Slide scions gently into the vertical incisions in the bark of the stock.

2. Use the spatula on the knife to peel back the edges of each cut.

5. As with cleft grafts, it is best to use raffia for binding the graft in place.

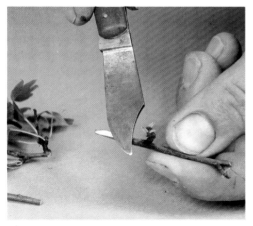

3. Trim scions to a taper so they make close contact with the cambium layer of the stock.

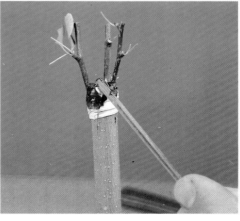

6. The graft should be covered with mastic, which helps healing and gives protection against parasites and disease.

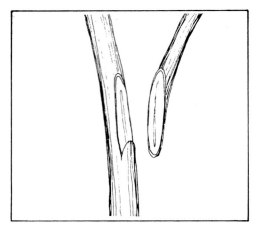

A side graft is easy to carry out and has a good chance of taking.

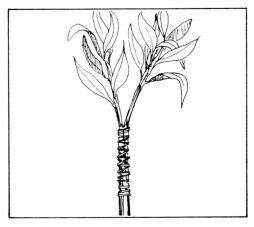

The side grafted scion is bound to the stock with raffia, but not sealed with mastic.

GRAFTING MASTIC

Contrary to popular belief, grafting mastic plays no active part in the 'taking' of a graft. This is proved by the fact that a number of grafts do not require sealing, the contact between cambium cells, which ensure a union, being enough just with binding. The addition of mastic is only needed where a large portion of tissue has been exposed and needs protecting from airborne diseases.

SIDE GRAFTING: Simple to carry out, side grafting entails making a slanting cut in the side of the stock into which the wedge-shaped end of the trimmed scion is inserted. The graft should then be bound and sealed with mastic.

This method is especially good for grafting conifers and evergreen trees. The cambium layers of scion and parent stock come into contact and this helps the graft to take.

BUDDING: This technique is very different from the others described, since it does not involve grafting a twig, but an eye or leaf bud attached to a small piece of bark. The bud is inserted into a T-shaped cut made in the bark. As with crown grafting take care not to damage the wood when doing this and use the knife's spatula end to open the bark a little. Insert the bud and then bind, but do not seal with mastic.

This method of grafting is probably gentler than the others for the stock, which is not damaged if the graft does not take. It can be carried out in summer when bud development is well advanced.

THE ADVANTAGES OF GRAFTING
As we have seen, grafting can be considered one of the most reliable methods of propagation. It also makes for a considerable saving in time, compared with raising from seed.

Grafting also offers the bonsai enthusiast other benefits, such as improving the shape of a tree. It is possible to use the bonsai tree's own branches to add a branch where one is missing. This takes grafting out of the realm of propagation and into that of bonsai shaping.

Grafting is also used to alter the gender of trees, making a sterile dioecious tree monoecious and fruit-bearing. It is enough just to graft a branch from a male tree on to a female one to provide for notably easier fertilization of the flowers.

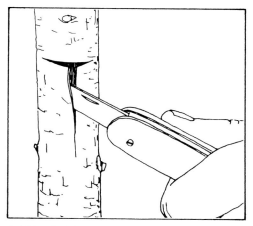

1. When budding make a T-shaped incision in the bark and carefully open the flaps.

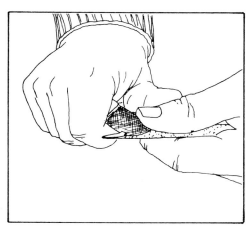

1. The English method or tongued approach graft consists of fitting the scion above parent stock to form an extension.

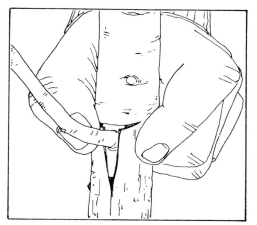

2. The bud – or as here a scion with a heel of older growth – is fitted into the T-shaped cut.

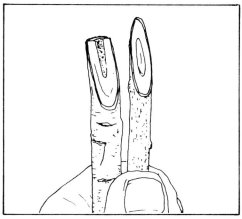

2. Stock and scion are trimmed to a taper, with the tip of the stock being lightly cut back.

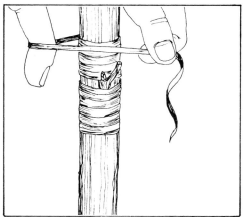

3. The bud graft (a bud with a heel of bark) is inserted, then held firm by binding. Mastic is not necessary.

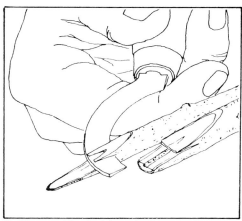

3. The matching incisions should make for a perfect connection. This graft is simply bound with raffia: sealing is not necessary.

TRAINING BONSAI

By definition, the perfect bonsai should have an aged-looking trunk and a vigorous growth of branches and leaves. The proportions of the tree should be similar to those of natural growing trees in the country or in forests but in miniature. Perfect results can only be obtained by continuous intervention. This will involve frequent pruning of the branches, leaves and roots, along with wiring, which moulds the trunk and branches into various accepted styles of bonsai. The following pages tell you how to shape your bonsai.

PRUNING

Whatever the growing technique, the purpose of pruning is always to control the growth of the tree by managing the development of branches, leaves and later its fruits (by thinning out). This is why pruning is so important throughout the life of the bonsai. As with fruit trees, we must distinguish between pruning to form the shape of the tree and on the other hand for its care and maintenance. Both need special equipment for the delicate operations involved.

Pruning equipment

A set of good scissors or clippers, both efficient and well designed, is essential to produce trees which conform to the aesthetics of bonsai.

Branches should be cut with a pair of strong cutters and sometimes (older branches, for instance), a pruning saw.

There are two types of scissors, those with strong, thick blades and large, broad handles and those with short blades and long, straight handles. The former are for cutting leaves and the latter for nipping buds.

The above are the general, all-purpose tools you should have for bonsai. As well

as these you should have wiring tools, which are described in detail on page 63.

Pruning for shape

To a large extent, the quality of a bonsai depends upon this. Pruning should be carried out very early on trees grown from seed or propagated vegetatively (from cuttings, grafting or layering). However, it can be done much later on a tree collected from the wild.

As a basic rule, always cut back one of

Like any good tree surgeon, you should have a complete set of tools.

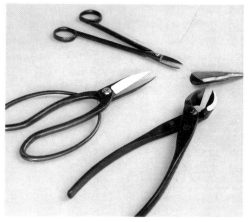

Bonsai pruning tools: *top*, bud clippers; *left*, ordinary scissors; *below*, branch cutters.

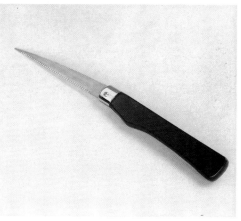

Knife-saw with fold-away blade: a must for cutting larger branches which cannot be cut with cutters.

Using a pointed saw. The cut should be neat and clean without splinters.

This badly placed branch should be removed with a pair of cutters.

The powerful curved blades of these cutters will ensure a very clean cut with a minimum of effort if you keep them sharp.

two opposite branches on the trunk. In this way, you will produce a tree with alternate branches in keeping with bonsai tradition. Beyond this simple fundamental rule, pruning for bonsai formation is intended to shape the tree to the form you want. Be discriminating when removing branches, since a branch cut from the trunk will not grow again and you may be left with an assymetrical or badly-shaped tree. Any error in your judgement may be rectified by grafting on a replacement branch – but this is always a delicate operation and not guaranteed to succeed. Although there are certain rules (such as systematic pinching out of the tips to obtain a well branched crown), this sort of pruning is generally a matter of common sense. It is obviously necessary to cut out suckers developing at the base of the trunk of a broom shaped tree, just as it is to cut back the leading shoot of a tree that you want to form a bushy shape, the skill being in selecting the right branch to take over as the new leader. Cuts should be clean, so the tree can heal quickly. This often means using a pair of cutters with slightly curved blades. For slightly thicker branches, the small hole left in the trunk should be filled with grafting mastic to accelerate healing and eliminate all traces of the scar where the bark has grown back. Where a pruning saw has been used, (here, a pointed, fine-toothed saw), it is almost always necessary to trim the cut with a pair of cutters or the blade of a grafting knife.

Tools should always be sharp and clean. Sterilize the blade with a flame after each pruning, to reduce the risk of transmitting viral diseases.

At this point, it might be useful to stress the quality of the tools you use. Traditional Japanese tools are certainly not cheap, but they are perfectly adapted to the requirements of bonsai cultivation. Do resist the temptation to use ordinary secateurs, or, for that matter, any other tools. You will only risk ruining your tree completely for the sake of a small outlay.

This lump, the result of a badly healed scar, should be removed with a pair of cutters.

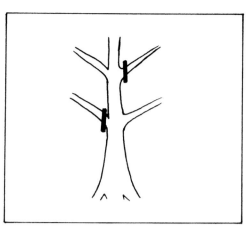

One of the basic rules of formative pruning is to remove one of each opposite pair of branches.

If the piece being removed is quite large, it is better to trim it several times.

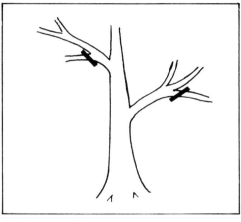

It is also a good idea to remove some of the branches that point downwards.

After performing 'surgery' in this manner, apply some mastic to the newly-made cut to prevent entry of bacteria.

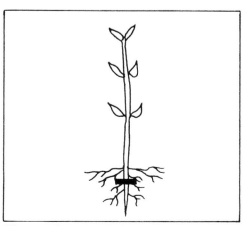

The central tap root of this young seedling destined to become a bonsai should be removed, to strengthen the lateral roots.

Formative pruning

Removing the tap root.   Pruning the main shoot.   Pruning the branches.

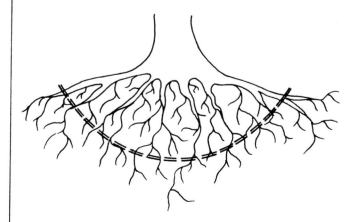

Root pruning

The various pruning operations shown in these diagrams will produce a well balanced broom-style bonsai, and is suitable for deciduous trees and, in particular, zelkova.

Maintenance Pruning

This is at least as important as formative pruning, since it also makes a day-to-day contribution to the effort of producing a bonsai of a particular style.

Maintenance pruning will vary, since any tree could be pruned several times during its growth. There are several different pruning methods that suit different species and cultivars of trees and you should follow the correct one.

In general terms, pruning for care and maintenance is intended to restrict the irregular growth resulting from the natural development of the tree. It is intended to promote harmony between the trunk and the branches and their foliage, which is essential to obtain a tree worthy of the name bonsai. Pruning for care and maintenance is repeated throughout the growing season to reduce the number of new branches by disbudding, to reduce the size of the leaves by trimming them and to shorten the shoots to inhibit their growth. This is an indication of the amount of care bonsai require for a large part of the year.

DEBUDDING: This type of pruning is only for deciduous trees. Pinch the buds out with your fingernails when the first growth appears. This is normally done at the beginning of spring, although it may be done several times during the year on some trees (e.g. elm, maple, hornbeam). When carried out repeatedly it produces smaller leaves. The tree may be affected to some degree and so should be fed regularly with modest amounts of fertilizer.

TRIMMING LEAVES: This mainly concerns trees with broad leaves, like chestnuts and oaks. Clip the leaves down by a half in late spring. Leaves clipped like this will drop off and be replaced with smaller leaves during the summer. Deciduous trees with small leaves can have their leaves completely removed (heavy pruning), the operation being repeated several times in the growing season. This is a radical practice which should only be carried out if the tree is quite healthy and vigorous.

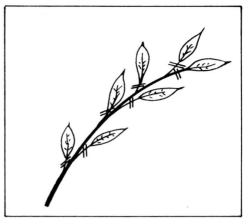

When removing whole leaves, leave a small part of the petiole, or leaf stem.

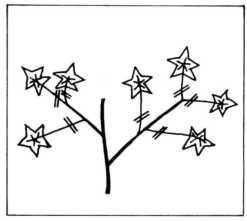

When clipping maple leaves, always retain a small part of the petiole.

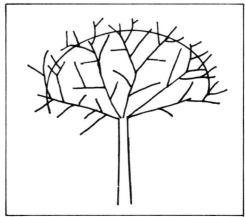

The diagram shows how you would cut back branches to obtain a rounded or broom shape to your tree. Careful cutting will give a better shape.

1. The luxuriant foliage of this *Zelkova serrata* needs pruning.

2. This zelkova is being methodically pruned with scissors.

CUTTING OR PINCHING BACK SHOOTS: The most important maintenance operation on bonsai, since the quality of the tree's foliage largely depends on this. Pinching back helps preserve shape, by inhibiting the natural exuberance of the growth. The method may differ from one species or cultivar to another, depending on whether the tree is deciduous or a conifer.

PINCHING BACK DECIDUOUS TREES: How often this is done depends on the growth rhythm of the tree. For a maple, it will be repeated several times in the season, whereas a hawthorn may require pinching back twice only, in early summer and early autumn.

The technique is roughly similar for all species. It consists of nipping the shoots above a leaf joint, always leaving a pair of leaves on the branch. This operation will allow the branch to ramify and at the same time dwarf the new leaves. This method also encourages good sap circulation, called upon by the requirements of the branch. It goes without saying that flowering or fruiting trees should not be clipped until after flowering or fruiting has finished.

Always collect the leaves you have cut. If you leave them lying around, the plant will look unkempt and the decomposing leaves will keep the soil damp and favour infection by fungal diseases.

3. Once it has been pruned, the good proportions of the tree are restored. Pruning can be done several times in the growing season.

Clipping a maple leaf: here, using the special leaf-cutting scissors which form part of the bonsai enthusiast's equipment.

The upright shape (*Chokkan*) of this beech is completely obscured by the growth of shoots.

Beech has the particular idiosyncracy that its dead leaves do not readily drop off.

The fine blades of these scissors allow very precise pruning required by this Chinese elm.

When the growing season starts it is possible to pinch out shoots with the fingers.

After pruning, the shape of the beech tree is restored without any need to cut back branch structure.

Beeches, maples and elms can be pruned as here by leaving two to four pairs of leaves on each branch.

1. The leaves of this Japanese maple (*Acer palmatum*) should be completely removed.

3. Remove all the remaining leaves with leaf-cutting scissors.

2. First of all, use scissors to remove the largest leaves from the tree.

4. The tree is now completely devoid of leaves. It will take several weeks to grow some more.

WATCH OUT

Take care not to hurt yourself, because some conifers, in particular, have very sharp needles. If you are late pinching back, the needles may have hardened and could hurt you. Be careful not to prick yourself. Where there is any risk of injury, use scissors rather than fingers.

5. After a few weeks, a new generation of leaves will appear. These leaves will be much smaller than the previous ones.

PINCHING BACK CONIFERS: While the reasons for doing this are the same as for deciduous trees, the technique is considerably different. First of all, it is carried out just once a year, generally in mid-spring, when the young shoots start to sprout. In most cases it is sufficient to remove one third of the shoot with the fingers. Do this by pulling lightly and the shoot should come away easily. Do not use scissors, for fear of cutting the ends of the remaining needles which could then turn yellow a few weeks later. Whereas a pine shoot should only be lightly pulled, it is necessary to twist shoots of a spruce as well. Unlike the other conifers, the juniper should be pinched right back throughout its growing season, which lasts from mid-spring until mid-autumn.

1. Young shoots of araucaria can simply be pinched back by hand.

2. However pinching the shoots could equally well be done with scissors.

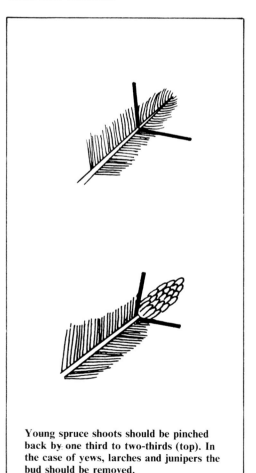

Young spruce shoots should be pinched back by one third to two-thirds (top). In the case of yews, larches and junipers the bud should be removed.

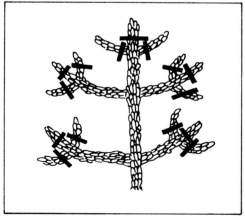

Diagram showing how a Chinese juniper should be pinched back. This should be carried out as required throughout its growing season.

Pinching back pine tree buds with the fingers by just nipping them out with your finger nails.

Juniper shoots being pinched back by hand – an operation which should be repeated regularly.

SOME EXAMPLES OF PRUNING AND PINCHING

Tree	Pruning or pinching technique	Time of year
Pinus thunbergii (Japanese black pine)	Prune the shoots	Early to mid-summer
Abies spp. and cvs. (spruce)	Prune half of all 2 cm ($\frac{3}{4}$ in) long shoots	As shoots appear
Juniperus chinensis (Chinese juniper)	Pinch out almost all shoots	Repeatedly from spring to autumn
Juniperus rigida var. *nipponica* (needle juniper)	Debud completely	As buds appear
Acer spp. and cvs. (maples)	Clip leaves (leave one pair at each point) and debud	Repeatedly from spring to the end of summer
Ulmus spp. and cvs. (elms)	As maples, above	As maples, above
Fagus spp. and cvs. (beech)	Prune branches and leaves, leaving one or two pairs	Repeatedly from spring to the end of summer
Fruit trees in general	Pinch back shoots to two buds after flowering	Mid-summer
Pyracantha spp. and cvs. (firethorn)	Pinch back new shoots, to two pairs of leaves	Mid-spring

WIRING

This is perhaps the most characteristic aspect of the art of bonsai, at least to the beginner. The necessity is born out of the need to modify the natural arrangement of branches to encourage them to grow to one of the classic styles.

Equipment

Essential equipment is brass or copper wire, occasionally steel wire (although rust may present a problem here) of different gauges. The thicker wire is used for the trunk and thinner wire for branches. To work it into position you will also need a pair of flat, long-handled, short-bladed pliers and a pair of wire cutters.

Though it is not strictly wiring equipment, the clamp, or 'trunk wrench', enables you to bend the trunk or larger branches to the required shape.

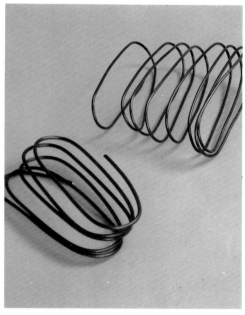

Copper or aluminium wire is available in various thicknesses. These metals do not rust.

Skilfully placed metal (preferably copper) wire can be used to shape the trunk and branches.

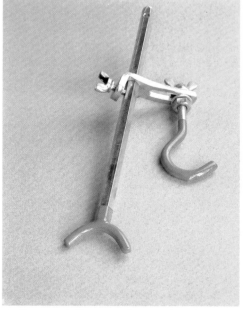

As its name indicates, a clamp or 'trunk wrench' serves to bend trunks and large branches to shape.

The technique

This consists of wrapping the length of metal wire spirally round the trunk or branch, working upwards from the lower end. This restrictive wrapping will enable you to obtain the shape you require. The wire should not be too tight, or it will cut off the sap flow and eventually strangle the tree.

This technique of shaping bonsai has developed relatively recently, but it is universally approved. However, you must be careful that it does not mark the bark or become embedded in the tree. For this reason it must be regularly removed and rewound.

Conifers should be wired at the end of the dormant period, usually in late winter. By contrast, deciduous trees should be wired in spring. Wiring should be left on conifers for five to six months and on deciduous trees for about eight to ten months, though there are no hard and fast rules. Keep a watchful eye on your bonsai, and remove any wires that threaten to mark the wood.

Metal wire is also used to brace the branches. That is, it is used to keep tension (generally downwards) on branches so that they maintain their direction of growth. Copper wire which is used for bracing should be anchored in the ground by a hook, or simply attached to the container. In some cases, the wire bracing may link the trunk and one branch.

Wiring is one of the bonsai styling techniques and not a part of the aesthetics of bonsai as many seem to think. Trees should therefore not be kept permanently wired, as if the wire had some significance in itself. Wiring is a rather clumsy method of shaping the tree, considered by some to be contradictory to the spirit of bonsai. It should be practised sparingly and only when absolutely necessary.

If you have inadvertently forgotten a wire and it has become embedded in the wood, do not try to remove it, as you will probably do more harm than good. Simply cut it off flush with the wood.

1. The metal wire should be wrapped spirally round the trunk and branches.

2. Snip off the end of wire with wire cutters, an essential piece of equipment.

3. Do not damage the branch when wiring. Make sure it is not wrapped round too tightly, as the branch will thicken as it grows.

4. Wiring makes it easy to bend the branches in the direction you wish.

7. *Right*: the tree before wiring and shaping; *left*: the tree after wiring.

5. The side shoots of the main branch can also be shaped in this way.

8. The wires on this *Acer trifidum* maple are clearly visible in winter.

6. A cascade style (kengaï) Chinese juniper (*Juniperus chinensis*) which has been formed by completely wiring the tree.

9. Steel wire on a *Podocarpus maki*. The wires on indoor bonsai should be replaced approximately every three to six months.

1. After six months to one year, the wiring of an outdoor bonsai should be removed.

2. Unwind the wire very carefully so as not to damage the bark.

3. As most of the tree is freed of wire the effect can begin to be appreciated.

4. The wire has now been completely removed and the tree has been given a lovely shape.

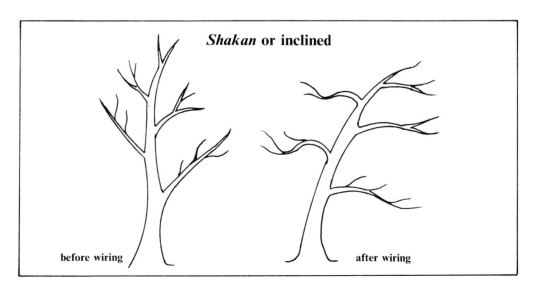

Shakan or inclined

before wiring

after wiring

Tips on wiring

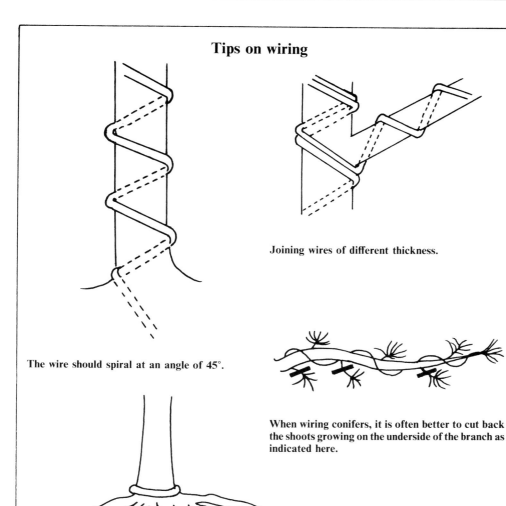

Joining wires of different thickness.

The wire should spiral at an angle of 45°.

When wiring conifers, it is often better to cut back the shoots growing on the underside of the branch as indicated here.

Wiring the base of the trunk. The purpose is to artificially thicken the trunk (see below). Do not make the wiring too tight.

AGEING

The 'jin' technique is peeling off the bark of a branch, polishing it and bleaching it with acid.

Jin carried out on almost the whole of the trunk of a juniper gives it the aspect of venerable old age. The effect of the dead wood is stunning.

It is every bonsai enthusiast's dream to own a very old tree, the fruit of several generations' labours. For those who cannot afford very old and costly specimens, it is useful to know that the aged appearance of a bonsai is not always the result of extreme age. There is a variety of simple techniques which you can use to age your bonsai. The main ageing technique is known as 'jin'.

The art of 'jin'

This is a technique which will give the trunk, or part of it, or a branch the appearance of dead wood, gnarled and smoothed by the passage of time. Peel back a strip of bark with a special scalpel (a jin scalpel), or a very sharp grafting knife. Then rub the wood with very fine grade sandpaper to polish it well. Then treat it with dilute citric acid or scouring solution, making sure that it does not penetrate the wood too deeply as it could poison the tree. This treatment will quickly bleach the wood giving it an old, seasoned appearance.

The jin technique is particularly suitable for conifers, which take on the aspect of trees weatherbeaten by wind and spray by the sea.

When trunk and branches are treated in this way, it is described as 'shari' and when the method is taken further still, to the point where the trunk is literally hollowed out, the method is known as 'sabamiki'.

The uninitiated may feel that the tree is being maltreated, but all trees treated in this way remain vigorous and healthy. The bark is not a living part of the tree, but a protective covering. However, a strip must always be left on as the cambium layer and the vessels carrying water and nutrients must be allowed to perform their tasks if the tree is to continue to flourish.

CARING FOR YOUR BONSAI

Bonsai are not just another kind of indoor or balcony plant. They demand constant and repeated attention – which is the price you pay to maintain these magnificent collector's plants.

If you are unable to look after your bonsai sometimes, do not worry: a fellow enthusiast is sure to help out or a professional bonsai nursery may well be happy to take in your plants and care for them in your absence: but you can be sure that they will still recognize you when you return!

REPOTTING

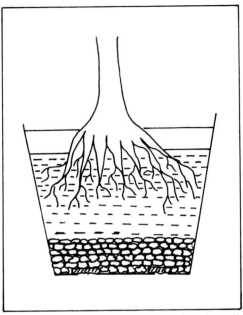

Make sure that your bonsai container is well drained, to prevent any possibility of root rot.

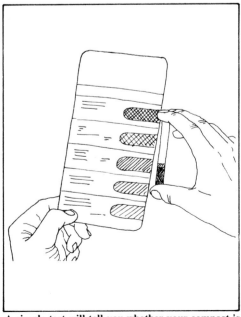

A simple test will tell you whether your compost is acid, alkaline or neutral (pH level). This gadget is sold in most garden centres.

Compost

Good quality compost is essential, since it has a direct effect on the health of the tree. Opinions on composition are divided, but as a general rule, a bonsai will thrive in compost made up of equal parts of good quality loam, peat and either sand or rotted turf. Some plants, such as rhododendrons and azaleas, need a lime-free or acid growing medium. The experts generally agree that the ideal mixture differs for deciduous trees, conifers and flowering trees. It is important to stick to the compost mixture in which the bonsai plant developed, so you should ask the grower about this when you buy your bonsai. The compost should always be sieved to eliminate any risk of damaging the roots.

Why repot?

This is an important matter, which is frequently neglected. Unlike a normal indoor or balcony plant, the bonsai needs a container in complete harmony with its size and style. Let us recall that in Japanese, the word *bonsai* means tree in a tray. Ignore this at your peril: you may end up with an aesthetic catastrophe and a spoiled bonsai.

There is an extensive range of bonsai containers, usually offered by the growers themselves. Most of these trays are of Japanese or Chinese origin. Flat trays are best suited to trees with a spreading or trailing habit, with slightly deeper trays for upright trees and even deeper trays for tall, slender or cascading plants. Forest or grove arrangements are most attractive displayed in very flat trays or even sometimes simply on stone slabs decorated with some rocks. Most bonsai trays are made of stoneware, either glazed or unglazed. They are seldom decorated and the most usual colours are blue, pale green and brown.

Below This group planting badly needs repotting. The large, flat tray shown in the bottom right hand corner is perfect. When the roots reach these proportions, urgent action is needed.

Pictured also are some of the trays available for bonsai. The specialists offer a wide range of them, giving you the chance of harmoniously matching your plant and its container.

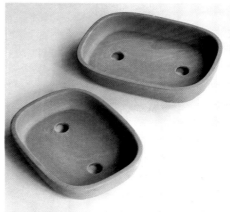

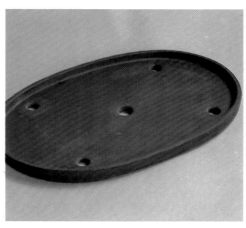

1. **Two tools essential for repotting: a small trowel and rake.**

Preparing the container

Bonsai trays have large drainage holes, through which any excess water from the frequent watering can drain, so that it does not stagnate and set up root rot. Do not cover these holes with a stone or piece of clay pot, as in normal plant pots. Use plastic mesh (which will not rot or rust), fixed in place with plastic coated wire hooked on to the outside of the tray. In this way, none of the finely sieved potting compost will leak out, even after generous watering. The plastic mesh also has the advantage of stopping unwanted visitors, such as the wood louse, from getting into the pot.

2. **This *Acer palmatum* is due for repotting. In the foreground are the necessary tools.**

4. **Plastic mesh should be placed over the drainage holes to prevent any soil leaking out.**

3. **This flat tray is ideal. It is considerably larger than the previous one. The drainage holes in the bottom should be left open.**

5. **Keep the mesh in place with plastic-coated steel wire. The advantage of using this wire is that it will not rust.**

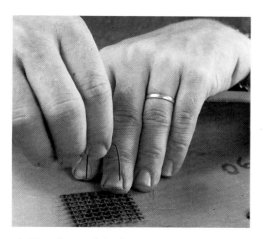

6. **Form hoops of plastic-coated wire and slot these into the mesh.**

8. **The pieces of mesh are held firmly in place over the drainage holes in the tray.**

7. **Place mesh over holes and hook wire ends under tray to secure in place.**

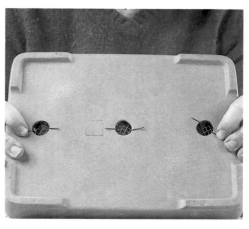

9. **The underside of the tray shows clearly how the wire keeps the mesh firmly in place.**

Removing it from its pot

It becomes necessary to change the pot or tray when the plant becomes 'pot-bound' by the growth of its roots. To remove the bonsai from its pot, stop watering until the compost is relatively dry, but at the same time make sure the plant does not suffer. Then gently lift the bonsai by its trunk: if the compost is dry, the plant should come out quite easily.

Check the soil

It is a good idea to check the soil for the sake of the tree's health. Check that the compost is not harbouring any undesir-

able creatures, such as ants, woodlice or insect larvae. You will also be able to monitor the root development and decide when to repot.

Root pruning

This is thought to be vital to the art of bonsai, root pruning directly helping to dwarf the tree. However, root pruning will also help to rejuvenate the tree by bringing the feeding roots a little nearer to the trunk.

Start by removing most of the earth from the old root ball by gently scraping with a special bonsai rake. This will also

10. If the earth is dry, the tree can be quite easily lifted from its tray.

untangle the roots. It should be done as gently as possible, avoiding damage to the roots (especially the larger ones) so far as practicable. Take a pair of wide-handled scissors and snip the roots down to about half their length. Remove completely any roots which do not seem healthy or which were damaged when the tree's roots were combed. Your tree is now ready for repotting.

Root pruning is a testing time for the bonsai tree: this is why it is vital that it takes place at the start of spring, when the tree is at its most vigorous. Water generously after repotting, then keep fairly dry until the tree is re-established.

11. Start by brushing away the earth with your hand to remove the drainage layer.

13. A metal rake will untangle the roots and the web of fibres in the root ball.

12. Continue removing earth with a wooden stick, taking great care as you do so that you do not damage the main roots of the tree.

14. This is how your tree should look after it has been removed from its pot and its roots have been untangled.

Repotting

We have seen how important it is to choose a container of the right size. When you have prepared the tray as described, spread a drainage layer of gravel or pebbles in the bottom. The potting compost should be sifted several times, with the coarsest material placed on top of the drainage layer, followed by successive layers of compost with the finest on top. Then plant your bonsai and add the very finest soil. If dry enough, the fine soil will easily filter down through the roots. Firm lightly before watering.

You may find it difficult to keep some

17. Sifting the potting compost. It should be similar to the type the tree was originally growing in.

15. Root pruning: this technique is vital in order to keep the tree miniature.

18. The largest particles will form the drainage layer in the bottom of the tray.

16. The roots were pruned by about two-thirds their length. The size of the root system is again in proportion with the top growth of the tree.

19. Spread the drainage layer evenly with the palm of your hand and firm it lightly. It will enable excess water to drain away.

20. The tree to be repotted should be placed more-or-less centrally in the tray – or so that it looks balanced and right.

21. Fill in the space between the plant's root ball and the tray with potting compost.

of the larger trees in place unassisted. Avoid using any kind of stake. Instead try keeping the tree's root ball in place with metal wire passed over the base and through the drainage holes. This is an efficient, invisible method. Do remember to remove the wire once the tree has taken root. The tray should be about three-quarters filled with compost, with a layer of very finely sifted soil to finish off the surface. Firm it down with the spatula at the other end of the bonsai rake or use tweezers. One can also cover the soil with a layer of moss which is decorative and serves to keep the soil moist after each watering.

Watering should be done slowly, continuing until excess water runs out of the drainage holes. This job can take a long time, since the compost used for repotting should have been very dry. To prevent moisture evaporating too quickly, put the bonsai where it is sheltered from wind and sun for several weeks. It should start to flourish in no time, overcoming the shock of being repotted. Never forget that repotting is always traumatic for the plant and act accordingly. It is also imperative to choose the right tray for transplanting the tree. If you change your mind after repotting is completed, it could do your bonsai irreparable harm to subject it to a second repotting after such a short time.

22. Pack soil between the root ball and the remaining soil with a wooden stick or spatula end of the bonsai rake so no air pockets are left.

23. Firm down the soil with the special trowel. This trowel should form part of your basic range of bonsai tools.

WATERING

A tree developing in its natural surroundings needs a considerable amount of water, which it obtains by developing deep roots which stretch far into the ground. A bonsai has similar requirements in proportion to its size. In other words, most bonsai need frequent and copious watering, particularly in summer. The fact that most bonsai are kept outside and exposed to the rain does not mean that one can dispense with watering since the moisture held by the root ball is always inadequate.

Water

Like other trees, bonsai need fresh water, free from toxic physical or chemical elements. Of course, the best water is rainwater, even though it may be polluted in towns. The ideal solution would be to collect rainwater in a water butt, but this is not always practical.

Well water is also suitable, provided it is not hard (i.e. limy), in which case water softening equipment should be used. Alternatively ·water softening tablets which are offered for sale can be added according to the instructions on the packaging to 'soften' the water by reducing the pH.

Tap water should only be used if relatively free from chemicals used in the purification process. The main danger is from chlorine, which is highly toxic to plants. If there is no alternative, keep the water outside in the open for several days, in which time much of the chlorine should evaporate. Whatever water you use – particularly if it is well water – make sure it is not too cold or it could give the plant a shock. It is a good idea to fill your watering can several hours before use, so the water can warm to the temperature of its surroundings.

How to water

Always water bonsai with a fine rose so you do not damage the delicate leaves or wash away the surface compost. If you only have a few plants a watering can with a fine rose will do. If you have a collection of some size, watering may become a major chore and you will need sprinklers, operated mechanically by a tap or automatically by an electronically controlled valve.

The traditional watering can, with long neck and rose remains basic equipment for watering bonsai. This one is designed for use in a greenhouse.

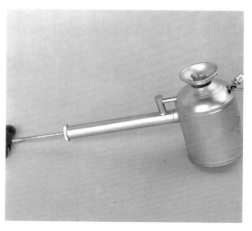

Leaves, sown seeds and young plants are best sprayed with a mister. The apparatus is worked by pressure or a pump.

1. **This multiple planting has reached a critical stage of dehydration.**

2. **Abundant watering is called for. As soon as the soil has absorbed the moisture, water again.**

As well as a watering can, you will need a sprayer, preferably a pressure sprayer, for misting over the leaves during warm weather. However, a sprinkler device will do this for you automatically.

It is impossible to say exactly how often bonsai should be watered, since each species has different requirements and climatic conditions may also vary. As a general rule of thumb, water often and sparingly, rather than occasionally and generously. The compost should be moist but not waterlogged. Any retention of water may set up root rot.

It is important to realize that bonsai require most water when growing most vigorously and in hot weather, and that less water is required in the weeks following root pruning, and clipping of shoots and leaves. This is because the reduced root system draws in less water and less is evaporated from the leaves.

In general terms, trees should be watered about once a week in winter, although this will depend on the overall humidity, and several times a day in midsummer. If the root ball dries right out, the tray should immediately be immersed in a basin of water. If you have to do this, be careful that the tree does not become uprooted. You should also damp over the foliage. It is especially important to look at the tree on a daily basis as the spring – and hence warmer weather – approaches.

Too much water can also be detrimental to the tree. For outdoor bonsai the heavy autumn and spring rains can be just as damaging as the hot summer sun. To stop the soil becoming waterlogged, we recommend placing a sloping shelter, such as a sheet of clear plastic or polythene, over the trees, or angling the trays slightly, so that excess water runs away on its own.

If the tray is left on a slant, watch that this does not result in the tree growing out of shape. Apart from water-loving trees such as wisteria and willow, do not stand the container in a tray or saucer, as this could stop water draining away and cause root rot.

Watering indoor bonsai poses fewer problems, since the indoor climate remains more or less stable. Water them at least once or twice a week, depending on the size of the pot (the smaller it is, the more often you will have to water it).

The leaves should be misted over with water frequently as the atmosphere can be very dry indoors. Central heating aggravates the problem still further, and you will find it necessary to spray even more frequently, especially in spring, when the growing season starts and often the heating is still on.

A practical precaution which is almost a necessity, is to place humidifiers on your radiators. This will prevent the air becoming too dry.

FEEDING

Besides taking water from the soil, the roots also absorb the nutrients needed to feed the plant. It is quite obvious that the small amount of compost in a bonsai tray is inadequate to supply enough nutrients to ensure the development and survival of the plant. So regular feeding with fertilizer is vital.

Which fertilizer?

It is hardly surprising that the bonsai tradition frowns upon the use of synthetic fertilizers, particularly liquid fertilizers and mineral-based powders. Apart from any consideration of dismissing them as 'modern', it should be noted that bonsai trees derive most benefit from slow-acting fertilizer, which means an organic fertilizer with a slow decomposition rate.

An ideal bonsai fertilizer contains about 50% nitrates, 30% phosphate, and 20% potash. It may be based on bonemeal, fishmeal, powdered horn or dried blood.

It may come in powder form and be sprinkled over the surface of the soil and raked in, or in the form of pellets, which are simply placed on the surface and absorbed by capillary action. The traditional preference is for pellets, but these cannot be used if the surface of the soil has a moss covering, which the pellets may 'scorch'.

There is no single rule about fertilizing. It is a little like watering, as amount and frequency depend entirely on the species of plant and size of tray. You should bear in mind that too much fertilizer does more damage to the plant than too little. Fertilizers are not intended to make bonsai grow, but to ensure their survival. Too much fertilizer may counteract the effort to dwarf the tree, besides which it may 'burn' the roots and lead to the death of the plant.

Organic fertilizer pellets can be obtained from specialist shops or some garden centres. Simply place them on the surface of the root ball.

Replace organic fertilizer pellets after a few weeks. This type of fertilizer is also available in liquid or powder form.

In the absence of special bonsai fertilizer, use an organic fertilizer such as dried manure.

Organic fertilizer contains a number of completely decomposed elements. Special European fertilizers, as pictured here and above, can be obtained.

Feed your plants during the tree's growing season, that is, from spring to autumn. Do not give flowering or fruiting trees any fertilizer until after they have flowered. For deciduous trees, continue feeding until the leaves drop, but conifers should not be given fertilizer after mid-autumn. If you use powdered fertilizer, two doses (two teaspoonfuls) per month should suffice. If you fertilize with pellets, wait until they have dissolved before replacing them and do not put the new pellets in the same places as the old ones. Always place the pellets about half way between the edge of the container and the trunk. Make sure, however, that they are slightly nearer the trunk, as they can damage the roots of the tree. Do not bother to feed in winter, when the roots absorb very little nutrients.

A foliar feed could be added to the water used to mist over the foliage. However, always use your discretion when tempted to use products advertised commercially for house plant care. Some products, such as leaf polishes, can prove harmful to certain types of plant. Do not confuse bonsai with indoor plants. Even though they are grown in rather similar ways, they need different care. Finally, note that indoor bonsai should not be given any fertilizer for three months after they have been repotted. With bonsai, you must be patient.

PRINCIPAL FERTILIZERS

Name	Formula	Effects
Nitrates	N	Promotes leaf and branch development, and growth in general.
Phosphoric acid	P	Enhances root and cell tissue development: regulates the reproductive activities (flowering and fruiting).
Potassium	K	Promotes production and circulation of sap, flowering and fruiting.

CHOOSING A BONSAI

Choosing a full-grown bonsai is always difficult – not least because of the cost involved. First decide where you are going to put your bonsai, whether indoors or outdoors, as this will directly determine your choice of bonsai. Think carefully how much time you will be able to devote to looking after your tree, and for outdoor bonsai, bear in mind as well the climatic conditions and how much exposure to light the trees will have. Always take advice from an expert, and read the following pages very carefully.

The magnificent silhouette of a 30-year-old *Juniperus chinensis* (Chinese juniper).

INDOORS OR OUTDOORS?

Two indoor bonsai of very different sizes: *left*, a tall, six-year-old cordyline; *right*, a ten-year-old tree, *Nandina domestica.*

Traditionally, bonsai trees come from the forests of the temperate humid regions of China and Japan, so are essentially outdoor plants. The idea of indoor bonsai came from the desire to keep bonsai in the home permanently, although tradition dictated that bonsai should only be brought indoors for special occasions, as when entertaining.

A temperate forest tree cannot tolerate the confined atmosphere of a house or flat. Conversely, tropical species which would thrive in this type of atmosphere are difficult to treat as bonsai. An exception to this is the fig tree, which, although of tropical origin, responds perfectly to miniaturization.

A number of species originating from mild climates (such as the Mediterranean coasts) can also be grown indoors, though they are generally thought of as cold greenhouse or conservatory plants. This applies to camellias and hibiscus.

This is a forty-year-old *Pinus parviflora*, which is one of the hardiest outdoor species which needs no protection from frost or sun.

This remarkable fig tree (60 years old) with its exposed roots can only live indoors, particularly in winter. It is a superb decorative specimen.

Outdoor bonsai

As we already know, this group makes up the majority of bonsai. Contrary to all appearances, a bonsai is no more delicate than its big brother in the forest. Neither rain, wind nor sun will harm it – provided it is adequately watered. Resistance to frost varies from one species to another, but as a rule all bonsai benefit from protection once the temperature drops below 5°C (41°F) and there is a risk of frost. Some trees, like the pines, firs, cedars, beeches, ginkgo or yews, need no more than a simple covering, such as a sheet of plastic, in a severe frost. Many others, like maples, elms and fruit trees in general, should be taken indoors into a cool room (10°C (50°F) maximum) when there is any danger of frost. All indoor bonsai can be taken outside, providing the temperature does not drop below 5°C (41°F). It is essential to protect the base of bonsai trees kept outside in winter and consequently, the tray itself, since the roots do not have a thick covering of earth to protect them. Simply use straw, or cover with leaves or peat.

DISPLAYING YOUR OUTDOOR BONSAI

The importance of bonsai presentation is obvious, since much of their charm lies in the harmony between the plant and its container. How you display your bonsai outdoors is equally important. Whether you use only a balcony or patio, or even a complete bonsai garden, it is vital never to stand the plant directly on the ground, unless it is a very old tree of considerable size. The ideal position is just below the line of vision.

Use stands that provide different levels and will let excess water drain away. Treat the wood with a non-toxic preservative to stop the wood rotting.

If using a window sill or balcony, make sure the pots are very stable, so that there is no danger of their falling over in a high wind. The higher the balcony the more problems can be caused by wind. The combination of high winds and hot sunshine can dry trees out very quickly. It is advisable to provide a strong windbreak and also to watch for rapid drying out.

In a garden, stands can be protected from the hot sun by a slatted shade made of plastic or wood. If you have a really extensive bonsai collection, try to mix the species and cultivars, to create an interesting and artistic display.

An outdoor bonsai garden should have one or more water connections, depending how large the garden is, since the trays do not contain much soil and so the trees risk drying out rapidly in summer. If you have a large collection, you should install a watering system with overhead pipes, with a succession of sprinklers set at regular intervals. Of course, the ideal is to install an automatic programming device which will control watering.

Where possible, avoid watering in broad daylight and exposing wet leaves to direct sunlight. This is where shading comes in useful. Bird droppings may also cause a problem. These can be prevented by fitting an awning with narrow slats. It is best to water first thing in the morning and then check again later in the day.

Outdoor displays look attractive when placed on slatted wooden staging. Here is an interesting group growing on a rock.

Conifers

These trees are named after their characteristic fruits, or cones. Most of them are evergreens, which gives them a constancy of form, regardless of season. This is not to say that they do not drop their 'leaves' – usually needles – although these are replaced at once by new growth, which is why these trees are always green.

Conifers lend themselves particularly well to bonsai treatment. Pines above all submit happily to pruning and their branches and trunks can easily be wired to form arching shapes. They can make spectacular specimens within a short space of time – within just a few years.

Conifers are generally hardy and therefore require a minimum of care. For this reason, they are good trees for the beginner to grow. In many cases, all you need do is pinch out the buds and shoots in spring and clear up the dead needles in autumn. They like a sunny position, but take care that the root ball does not dry out. (Most conifers originate from the drier regions of the world and do not need a great deal of water).

The bark of old conifer trees should be regularly scraped, since it often harbours parasites – a common example is overwintering greenfly eggs.

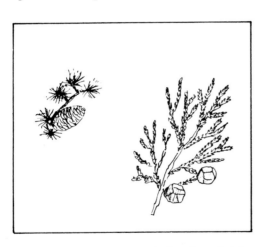

Left, drawing of the fruit (cone) of a cedar and *right*, chamaecyparis fruits.

Group comprising *left* a *Pinus parviflora* and, *right*, a *Carpinus japonica*.

Almost upright 40-year-old *Pinus thunbergii*. This is one of the easiest conifers to grow.

Juniper on a rock. It takes a classic shape which is particularly effective as a bonsai.

CONIFERS

Species	Description	Pruning	Pinching
Abies alba (silver fir)	Short, spiky evergreen needles, upright cones	spring, before bud burst	Early summer (two thirds of the shoots)
Cedrus spp. (cedar)	Short, spiky evergreen needles, dark green	spring, before bud burst	Late spring – mid-autumn (two thirds of the shoots)
Chamaecyparis spp. and cvs. (false cypress)	Evergreen, habit varies; slow developer	spring or autumn	All year round (two thirds of the shoots)
Cryptomeria japonica (Japanese cedar)	Slow developing evergreen; green foliage turns red-bronze in autumn	spring	Late spring – early summer (at the third node)
Juniperus chinensis (Chinese juniper)	Leafy evergreen, sea green in colour	spring, autumn	Early spring – early autumn (two thirds of the shoots)
Juniperus rigida var. *nipponica* (needle juniper)	Narrow, sharply pointed evergreen needles; cones blue, green or reddish	spring	Early spring – early autumn (drastic)
Larix spp. and cvs. (larch)	Deciduous needles, pale green in spring, turning darker in summer and gold in autumn	spring, before bud burst	Summer
Picea spp. and cvs. (spruce)	Erect evergreen needles, pendant cones	spring, autumn	Early spring – mid-summer (debud if growth is luxuriant)
Pinus parviflora (Japanese white pine)	Small fine bluish green needles	spring, autumn	Debud in late spring
Pinus thunbergii (Japanese black pine)	Strong, robust dark greyish-green needles	spring, autumn	Summer (remove shoots completely)
Taxus baccata (yew)	Blunt evergreen needles, dark green; bright scarlet 'berries' (arils)	spring, before bud burst summer	Late spring – early summer (reduce number of shoots)

Deciduous trees

These will be familiar as the trees of our temperate forests. The leaves fall in autumn at the end of an active season of growth which commences in early or mid-spring, depending on the species.

Almost all deciduous trees can be used for bonsai, but the most suitable are maples, beeches, hornbeams and elms, which lend themselves particularly well to leaf and shoot pruning. Most of the species originating in the Far East have, by nature, the added advantage of very small leaves. All deciduous trees colour in autumn. This can give a magnificent effect with colours ranging from gold to scarlet – a special bonus which makes up for their nakedness in winter.

Accustomed to our temperate climates, deciduous trees are easy to grow, provided they are watered adequately and kept out of hot sun. Their vigorous growth means that one must continually keep their shoots within bounds, with repeated pinching out to ensure the miniaturization of the leaves. Skilful pruning during dormancy will make precise shaping possible.

Deciduous trees are ideally suited for various multiple group arrangements, in trays or on a large stone slab, a quiet and elegant way of displaying such trees.

Two quite different leaves: *left*, hornbeam and *right*, birch, with catkins.

Zelkova serrata, or Japanese grey bark elm, in winter, clearly revealing the branch structure.

Acer palmatum, **45 years old. This maple is particularly well suited to bonsai treatment because of its naturally small leaves.**

The spectacular autumn colouring of a maple, showing off its delicate palmate leaves perfectly just before they drop.

A SELECTION OF DECIDUOUS TREES

Species	Description	Pruning	Pinching
Acer buergeranum (*A. trifidum*) (Trident maple)	Green dentate leaves, turning bright orange in autumn	Spring for branches, before bud burst. Autumn for leaves	Throughout the growing season
Acer palmatum and cvs. (Japanese maple)	Tiny dentate leaves with 5 or 7 lobes, turning bright red or orange in autumn	Spring, before bud burst	Throughout the growing season
Betula nigra (black birch)	Pale green foliage; reddish brown trunk with white base, bark flaking off in sheets	Spring, before bud burst	Throughout the growing season to 3 buds
Carpinus laxiflora (hornbeam)	Very luxuriant foliage produced in spring	Spring, before bud burst	Throughout the growing season to 2 buds
Fagus crenata (beech)	Crenate leaves, which turn brown in autumn but do not fall until spring	Spring, before bud burst, or autumn	Late spring and early summer, to 2 or 3 buds
Ginkgo biloba (maidenhair tree)	Two-lobed, fan-shaped leaves, green in summer, turning yellow in autumn	Spring, before bud burst	Throughout the growing season, cut back to 2 or 4 leaves, depending on the age of the tree
Malus cerasifera (Nagasaki crab apple)	Covered in blossom in the spring. Small apples can follow flowers if pollinated. Leaves somewhat large	After flowering. In autumn, prune back to a flower bud	Only pinch out very long growth through the growing season
Ulmus parvifolia (Chinese elm)	Tiny glossy leaves, cracked, flaking bark	Spring, before bud burst	Throughout the growing season
Zelkova serrata (grey bark elm)	Tiny oval leaves, spreading branches, luxuriant foliage	Spring, before bud burst	Throughout the growing season to 1 or 2 buds

Ornamental shrubs

The group of ornamental shrubs includes any shrub which is decorative by dint of its leaves, flowers or fruit. The species may vary considerably, since all they need to have in common is their decorative appearance.

We should differentiate between winter, spring or summer flowering shrubs, those producing fruit similar to that of normal fruit trees, such as the apple, and those with brightly-coloured, purely ornamental berries.

Growing methods can differ considerably, as do the pruning methods. In general terms, early flowering shrubs (some with flowers appearing before the leaves) should be pruned as soon as the blooms wilt, whereas later flowering shrubs (late spring or summer) should be pruned in winter, or before growth begins in spring.

Flowering or fruiting is always spectacular on bonsai, because of the profusion of tiny flowers and fruit, and their dwarf size, less noticeable than that of the leaves.

The majority of ornamental bonsai shrubs are outdoor kinds, but some of those originating from the Mediterranean area should be protected from frost in winter.

Cotoneaster (left) is often confused with pyracantha (right), though they are quite different.

Cotoneaster is prized for its decorative fruit and its foliage, which turns red in autumn.

Valued for its attractive white or pink flowers in spring, a crab apple tree produces tiny decorative apples in autumn.

An azalea in bloom is one of the most magnificent sights in bonsai. It demands good acid, peaty heathland soil.

A SELECTION OF ORNAMENTAL SHRUBS AND TREES

Species	Description	Pruning	Pinching
Azalea	See *Rhododendron*		
Camellia japonica (Japanese camellia)	Glossy evergreen leaves, flowers from mid-winter to spring	Spring, before the new leaves appear	Throughout the growing period
Cotoneaster horizontalis	Small glossy leaves, green, turning red in autumn, red berries, upright habit	Spring, before bud burst	At the start of summer to two or three buds. Trim long shoots in autumn
Crataegus spp. and cvs. (hawthorn)	Thorny, with small dentate leaves and white, pink or red flowers and decorative fruits in summer	Spring, before bud burst	At the start of summer to two or three buds. Trim long shoots in autumn
Jasminum nudiflorum (winter jasmine)	Green, square-section branches with cascading habit and a profusion of yellow flowers in winter	Early spring, just after flowering	After flowering; also reducing excessively long shoots in autumn
Malus spp. and cvs. (Crab apple)	Shiny oval leaves, flowers ranging from white to deep pink, cherry-sized red fruits	Spring, before bud burst	Reduce shoots in early summer, shape in autumn, prune in winter
Prunus mume (Japanese apricot)	Small, oval leaves, slender growth, bright pink flowers in winter	Spring, just after flowering	After flowering, and with limited trimming in summer
Prunus amygdalus (almond)	Pointed, slightly dentate leaves, white flowers in winter	Spring, just after flowering	After flowering
Prunus serrulata and cvs. (Japanese cherry)	Oval leaves, white to pink flowers mid to late spring	Spring, after flowering	After flowering, then throughout the growing season to two or three buds
Pyracantha angustifolia (firethorn)	Thorny, with evergreen pointed leaves; white flowers in summer; yellow, orange or red autumn fruits	At the end of winter	Late spring, then excessively long shoots in winter
Rhododendron spp. and cvs.	Shiny pointed evergreen leaves, profusion of flowers in late spring	Just after flowering	In summer remove faded flowers; trim long shoots
Wisteria spp.	Pale mauve flowers in hanging clusters in late spring	Early spring, preserving the young shoots	Remove excessively long shoots in late summer

1. The tropical Ficus is one of the easiest indoor bonsai plants to grow.

2. As spring comes to an end, prune all the leaves from the fig.

Indoor bonsai

Traditionally, a bonsai tree is an outdoor plant, however, quite recently, efforts have been made to find species and cultivars that will thrive in the confined atmosphere of the home. Most indoor bonsai are, in fact, of tropical origin, trained to create the traditional shapes of outdoor bonsai.

Choose plants which become woody enough to be treated as bonsai.

While taking the origins of the plant into account, stand it in a well-lit place, since lack of light is one of the most frequent causes of failure.

These plants need to be warm by day (about 15°C/60°F), but cooler by night. It is vital to recreate the humid conditions of their regions of origin, which are far from likely in winter in our often dry and overheated homes. It is essential to spray the leaves generously and often. With some bonsai it could be beneficial to stand the container on a tray filled with moist gravel to keep the air around it humid all the time. But never stand your bonsai container in a saucer or tray filled with water, as this could rot its roots.

For a large bonsai collection, the perfect solution is a heated greenhouse equipped with a sprinkler system, able to keep an ideal level of humidity.

3. The ficus, from which all the leaves were cut, will quickly grow new ones smaller than the first.

The exposed roots of this *Ficus* make a particularly effective display when trained in this swirling shape.

Bambusa ventricosa makes an original indoor bonsai. Here a shoot is being pruned.

Having trimmed back the smaller shoots it is time to tackle the main subject.

The bamboo after its branches have been pruned and its leaves pinched back.

Pinching out young bamboo shoots in spring.

Care of indoor bonsai

Apart from needing the best possible growing conditions (such as good light in a warm, draught-free position away from direct heat), indoor bonsai need quite different attention from their outdoor cousins.

Most require repotting every two years, preferably in spring. They *can* be potted at other times of the year, but it is best to provide some bottom heat to encourage re-rooting. Repotting should be accompanied by root pruning ($\frac{1}{3}$ to $\frac{2}{3}$, depending on growth). As with outdoor bonsai, try and stick to the same shape container, but of larger size. The drainage holes should be big enough to prevent any waterlogging which could cause root rot.

Do not use organic fertilizers as for outdoor bonsai, but use liquid fertilizers like those recommended for ordinary houseplants. Because bonsai containers are shallower than normal indoor plant pots, dilute the fertilizer further to avoid any risk of concentrated liquid damaging the roots.

Feed indoor bonsai with fertilizer in small, frequent doses (about once every three weeks), but do not feed in winter, unless the tree is being kept warm and is still growing vigorously.

Pruning and pinching

Indoor bonsai also should be pruned and pinched back regularly to obtain the required shape, preferably in spring, before the season's growth begins.

Shoots and leaves should be pruned and pinched back throughout the growing season, as soon as the shoots become too large. In some cases, such as with ficus, all the leaves should be cut back. However, the latter should only be carried out in late spring.

Training

Wiring is nearly always necessary to train indoor bonsai. The method is similar to that used for outdoor bonsai, but the wires should be removed every three to six months at most. However, there are some indoor bonsai, like bamboo, that cannot be wired.

Ficus are a particularly suitable type of tree for growing over rocks with their

A podocarpus, more unusual than a ficus, also makes a fine indoor bonsai.

roots exposed. They are planted over the chosen rock in exactly the same way as an outdoor tree such as a trident maple. In time, you will find that the roots thicken and intertwine, growing to form attractive interwoven patterns.

A SELECTION OF INDOOR BONSAI

Species	Description	Pruning	Pinching
Camellia japonica and cvs. (Japanese camellia)	Shiny evergreen leaves, pink to red flowers appearing from early winter to early spring	Summer, preserving the flower buds	Pinch leaves back after flowering
Ficus (many)	Glossy evergreen leaves; choose those with very small foliage	Summer	Constantly, remove all leaves in early summer
Gardenia jasminoides (Gardenia)	Oval evergreen leaves, richly scented white flowers	Spring, before bud burst	After flowering and in mid-summer, to two or three buds
Podocarpus	Evergreen, very thin leaves	Spring, before bud burst	Late spring and early summer
Serissa japonica (thousand star tree)	Slender, oval evergreen leaves	At any season	After flowering

HEALTHY BONSAI

Bonsai are sensitive trees, demanding more care and precision in pruning, training and repotting than any other plants. The very restricted environment they have to live in makes them particularly susceptible to pests and diseases. Preventive treatment helps, and a constant watchful eye should be kept on your bonsai to catch any infection at the earliest stage and eradicate it with the right treatment. These dangers are compensated for by the fact that all bonsai are trees or shrubs, and so by nature are robust.

PREVENTIVE TREATMENT

Sweep away the leaves after pruning. A compact, traditional brush should be part of every bonsai enthusiast's tool kit.

Cleaning

Bonsai are particularly prone to attack by a variety of pests and diseases. This problem is exacerbated by the very restricted habitat in which they are grown. Because of their reduced size, they are more drastically affected by pests than their giant brothers in the forest. Yet it cannot be said that bonsai growing techniques actually aggravate the situation (except with greenhouse-grown tropical plants). The most effective preventive treatment is regular cleaning of the plants, to avoid creating conditions favourable to pests and diseases.

After pruning or pinching, make sure that the earth around the base of the trunk is free of leaves and other plant debris. Otherwise the debris is likely to decompose and create just the right conditions for fungal diseases or moss, which set up root rot. This will eventually lead to the death of the tree.

Use a spatula very carefully to scrape the bark of the tree. The bark can harbour insect pests and their eggs or larvae.

Moss which grows up the trunk or trunks can easily be brushed away, as shown here, with a hard nylon toothbrush.

You can buy purpose-designed brooms to sweep away the debris.

Though decorative to look at, moss forms a good refuge for pests and their larvae. It is for you to decide whether its decorative value outweighs any threat it poses to your bonsai.

If you decide in favour of moss growing on the soil, keep it well away from the trunk and branches. Use a special spatula or a hard nylon toothbrush to scrape away unwanted moss. In any case, thin out the moss on a regular basis. A close relative of moss is liverwort. In all instances this should be removed from the soil surface and thrown in the rubbish bin afterwards. If you just allow it to fall on the ground it will re-root and the spores will soon find their way back to the trees. With a few exceptions (mentioned later), take care not to damage the bark or cut into the wood.

Use insecticide to treat any larvae or greenfly you spot in the moss.

You may feel that grass around the base of the tree looks very attractive, but do remember that, besides the risk of pests and diseases, grass can take nutrients from the soil to the detriment of your bonsai. It is a good idea to weed through occasionally, and also aerate the surface soil.

Use a pair of special tweezers to remove any weeds. This is vital equipment for the enlightened bonsai grower.

Besides these preventive treatments, keep a constant eye on the plant and check the state of the leaves particularly looking underneath the leaves and the trunk, since pests may lurk in the bark.

If you find greenfly or larvae, treat with insecticide at once. Scrape away any loose bark from older trees, which may have started to flake off. If you find dead wood in the bends of any of the branches, or in any holes or cavities, remove it with the aid of a scalpel (like those used for jin techniques), cutting down to the live wood, which should then be protected with mastic to help it heal. This may appear drastic, but it is the only way to stop the rot spreading.

Weeds can easily be removed from the surrounding soil with tweezers.

The same tweezers can be used to remove liverwort that is spreading where it is not wanted.

Liverwort has a very simple, primitive root system. It is not always removed, and can be used for decoration around a bonsai.

PESTS

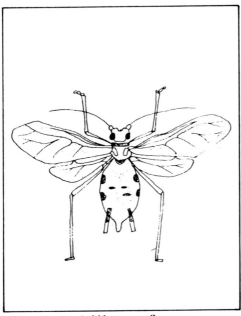

Aphid or greenfly

Caterpillar

Like all plants, bonsai can fall prey to a number of parasites, which feed off the sap, at the expense of the tree. These pests benefit from the regular watering and health care given to bonsai. The following are some common pests, although indoor bonsai can be susceptible to attacks by white fly as well.

Aphids (greenfly)

As most gardeners will know, these pests are hard to eliminate. They are small, green, yellow or brown insects which live in colonies on the leaves and stems. Extremely prolific, they quickly multiply to form clusters that cover the whole plant. They weaken the tree by sucking its sap and also encourage fungal and viral diseases, which move in quickly when the plant is weakened. These also attract ants which establish their nests in the root ball.

Aphids can be quite easily eradicated by spraying with insecticide. Old bark should be scraped, as it often harbours insect eggs.

One of the most persistent of aphids is the woolly aphid. This has a white fur coat which protects the aphid from contact with insecticide. Although systemic insecticide should control this pest, a better method is to paint it with methylated spirit. If your tree looks as though it is developing tiny pieces of cotton wool, then it has woolly aphid.

Caterpillars

There are many different kinds of caterpillars, all with a voracious appetite for foliage, which attack plant leaves, to the point of total destruction.

Some of them develop in cocoons on the undersides of leaves before appearing in the daylight. They twist themselves into silky webs, hence their name, tortrix caterpillars. Sometimes they develop in the leaf and flower buds.

Caterpillars are not always easy to eliminate, as they are sometimes resistant to insecticides. Remove them by hand where you see them and destroy them. An insecticide powder, which stays on the leaves longer, can give good results, as the caterpillars absorb it as they eat their way through the leaves. It may be possible to catch some species in a saucer of glue placed at the base of the tree. This will prevent moths from climbing the tree at night in autumn and laying their eggs on the leaves.

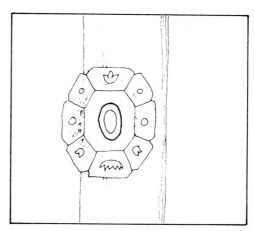

Scale insect

Scale insects
Minuscule insects which cling firmly to branches and trunk, protected by a scaly outer shell. These insects are destructive pests. The female penetrates the plant's skin and sucks out sap. Like aphids, they encourage the spread of fungal and viral diseases. Control with an oily insecticide in winter, then scrape away any dead bark. Eggs will continue to develop under the shells of dead insects. It is vital to burn all debris from the scraping.

Another method is to dip a small paintbrush or cotton bud in methylated spirit. This can then be painted on and around the scale.

Insect larvae
Some insects may lay eggs in the bonsai compost, that is, in the root ball. The larvae which hatch are especially fond of young roots, which they devour, depriving the plant of nourishment. So keep a watchful eye open during repotting, when you can destroy larvae with your fingers. You could also use a suitable insecticide like HCH.

Red spider mites
For long mistakenly thought of as insects, red spiders are actually mites, about which relatively little is known, due to their microscopic size. Though tiny, red spider mites are visible to the naked eye because of their bright colour. The tetranychus group are particularly voracious, the adult mite piercing the backs of the leaves to suck out the sap. They most frequently attack conifers, the needles of which then turn yellow and drop.

Mites are quite resistant to insecticides (which are formulated to kill insects, but not necessarily mites). Special products are hard to find. The most effective treatment is to prune away and burn infested branches.

Ants
Ants are formidable pests in several ways. Due to their fondness for aphids, on whose excretions they feed, they can almost be said to 'farm' them, since they convey them from one plant to another plant and protect them from predators such as ladybirds. In order to be near their food, ants also tend to congregate in nests in the soil around the roots, causing havoc in the root system and cutting through roots as they carve out tunnels. The sole remedy is to set a trap for them on the surface of the root ball.

If an ant's nest is set up in the root ball, the only solution is to lift the plant from its tray. Brush off the soil and eliminate as many larvae as possible. When disturbed, ants are easily dislodged.

DISEASES

Powdery mildew is a fungal disease which covers the whole plant in a downy white deposit.

Many treatments, whether insecticides or fungicides, can be sprayed on with a good vaporizer which gives an even spray.

This heading covers a number of problems which can affect the life of a plant, causing it to wither and eventually die. We generally distinguish between fungal diseases, deficiency diseases caused by an imbalance in plant nutrients, and bacterial and viral diseases (the latter usually incurable and fatal to the infected plant).

Although fungal growth is looked on with misgiving, it should be remembered that some fungus is not only harmless but beneficial. For instance, fine white mycelium growing around the roots should be encouraged as it is in certain cases a sign of good health.

Powdery mildew

This is certainly the most widespread fungus disease. It shows itself in the form of a white, floury layer which gradually spreads over the shoots and leaves.

The mycelium (equivalent to a root system) of the fungus draws sap directly from the plant's cell tissues which subsequently die. This fungus generally thrives in a hot, humid, poorly ventilated atmosphere and is encouraged by an excess of nitrogen.

Some specific treatments are available to deal with this fungus, most of them sulphur based. Use them to prevent the disease, especially where conditions favour the development of the fungus. Be careful not to wet the foliage over much, as this is a frequent cause of mildew.

Rust

Another common fungal disease, which occurs in the form of orange or brown patches or even blisters spreading over the underside of the leaves, which curl up and eventually drop. These patches and blisters result from infection by the Phragmidium fungus, which also thrives in a hot, humid atmosphere. Rust growth is commonly encouraged by an excess of potassium.

Black spot

Black spot is another formidable fungus, which mostly attacks the leaves (elms being particularly susceptible). The leaf becomes progressively covered in black patches, until it eventually shrivels and falls off.

Preventive treatment with a general fungicide is usually sufficient to deter black spot. If you discover it has attacked your plant, use a sulphur or mancozeb based product.

Chlorosis

This is one of the commonest deficiency diseases, caused exclusively by a shortage of iron in the plant nutrients. The leaf blade or needles turn yellow, while the veins usually remain green. Chlorosis generally occurs in chalky or limy soil, which locks up the iron. The best remedy then is to change the potting compost when repotting. Iron can also be given in liquid form, by adding sulphate of iron to the water when watering.

Other deficiency diseases

Potassium deficiency can kill off the leaves, which turn yellow at the edges, shrivel and finally drop.

Shortage of nitrogen hinders photosynthesis resulting in the leaves turning pale, with brownish patches appearing on the stalks of plants.

Magnesium deficiency can depress flowering, which becomes rather sparse. This deficiency also causes a slight yellowing of the leaves.

Phosphorus deficiency also restricts flowering and the leaves, though remaining green, fall prematurely.

All these deficiency diseases can be easily cured by a balanced feeding programme. This is why the choice of the right fertilizers is so important.

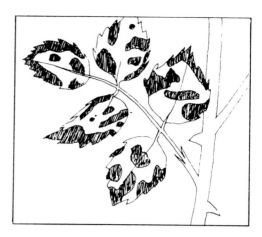

Black spot is a fungal disease which attacks the leaves of the plant.

Some treatments should be given as a powder, rather than a liquid spray. Here, a powder dispenser.

Your choice of fertilizer should take into account the precise needs of the individual tree, with special reference to the growth cycle of the tree.

Mildew

This fungal disease shows itself as a greyish mould on the undersides of the leaves and on the sepals of the flowers, marking them with a brown halo.

Good ventilation and careful watering usually suffice to put an end to this trouble. If this is not enough, use a suitable fungicide, preferably in powder form, to destroy the fungus.

With most fungal control, prevention is better than cure. For instance, although powdery mildew is treated by simple methods, it can be very persistent. Therefore start treating potential mildew victims before the mildew appears.

Root rot

This serious fungal disease affects only the roots. It is most often caused by contamination from poorly decomposed organic fertilizer used straight on the roots (fresh manure, for example). The fungus is encouraged by over generous watering, poor drainage and by standing the container on a tray or saucer.

As root rot affects the underground part of the plant, it is difficult to treat. If you are worried, you should examine the roots carefully when lifting or repotting the bonsai. It is hard to combat root rot. The best way is to remove all infected roots, which could itself have grave consequences for the bonsai, as the imbalance between roots and top growth could kill it. Lift the plant and brush away all contaminated soil as quickly as possible. After transplanting in fresh compost, spray the foliage well to compensate for the water the plant roots are unable to provide.

Canker

This is a bacterial rather than a fungal disease, which shows as swelling of the bark and callosities. It often arises after pruning with tools that have not been sterilized after cutting infected material (which shows the wisdom of passing the blades of a grafting knife or secateurs through a flame). The only effective way of controlling canker is to cut out infected areas – cutting away a branch or removing infected tissue. Be careful to dress the wounds made in this way with mastic to help them heal and to exclude further infection. It is vital to burn all diseased wood immediately and to sterilize the tools you have used.

Viral diseases

These are, fortunately, seldom encountered, for one can only control this trouble by destroying infected plants to stop the disease spreading to other plants and becoming an epidemic.

The most dangerous viral disease of cultivated plants is without doubt mosaic, which appears as a mottling – alternate green and yellow stripes or other shaped areas – on the leaves, and by a highlighting of the leaf veins. The leaves eventually shrivel, dry up and fall.

Control materials

The chemical products used to control these diseases are offered either as dilutable liquids (or powders to be dissolved in water), or as powders to be used in that form. So you need a sprayer and a powder blower as well.

The sprayer is also valuable for damping over the plants' foliage as necessary, so it is an indispensable item of equipment. A powder blower, on the other hand, is used less frequently, and only in special situations. What is more, some products which are offered in powder form can only be used when conditions are right for dusting.

BONSAI CALENDAR

MID- TO LATE WINTER

The branches have lost their leaves. Use this opportunity to examine the bark.

The first severe cold spells are likely in mid-winter and with them the danger of frost. Their effects will depend on the force and direction of the wind and the nature of one's trees.

The wet and dry thermometer shown on page 14 can provide a fairly accurate frost forecast, though keeping informed via the media, particularly television, probably provides a more reliable forecast as the satellite charts can be followed.

Bonsai trees kept outdoors should not be watered when it is severely cold as a moist root ball can freeze as soon as the temperature drops below 0°C (32°F). The small amount of compost in the bonsai tray, as in the illustration, puts trees at risk from frost that would not be if grown normally. But this does not mean that a bonsai will always die if it is slightly frozen.

However, if the temperature drops below −5°C (23°F), all trees at risk from freezing should be protected or brought indoors. If the trees are kept indoors during the winter, take steps to ensure that the ambient temperature does not exceed 5°C (41°F). All plants must be sprayed with water regularly. Their root balls can be protected by putting the trees side by side in a large box and covering their root balls with peat, making sure that they are well drained to reduce the risk of fungal diseases. If it snows, you must remove any snow from the branches at once, to prevent them being broken or deformed, thereby cancelling out the benefits of wiring.

Take particular care to protect bonsai trees kept close beside your house from the risk of snow falling from the roof during a thaw and causing them damage. On the other hand, watch that the trees do not receive too much winter sun, which can stimulate early buds which could then be damaged by late frosts. Premature budding can also upset the sap circulation, as the roots are still in very cold soil. Fertilizers should not be used during the winter while plants are dormant. Manure would either be completely ineffective during this dormant period, or even harmful during a sudden bout of warm weather, giving rise to premature budding.

Watering should only be done when strictly necessary as waterlogged soil freezes easily.

Winter is a good time for preventive treatment against fungal diseases and pests whose eggs and larvae spend the winter under the bark.

It is also a good time to choose a deciduous tree, since, bare of leaves, its shape is clear and defects easy to spot.

Late winter is a good time to prune all plants which must be shaped before they make new growth. However, do not touch spring flowering shrubs.

EARLY SPRING

This is a period of dramatic change for plants, a transition from the rigours of winter to the milder temperatures of spring. Early spring is a hazardous time when there is still a risk of severe frost, particularly at the beginning of the month, at a time when the young buds may have started to grow after a mild winter. Watch out for any serious changes in the weather, bearing in mind that winter is hardly out of the way yet.

Watering is a skilled operation at this time of year, as budding plants require a lot of water, but this puts their root balls at risk from frost if the temperature drops sharply. During this period, it is well worth protecting trees at night and when the weather is overcast and then placing them in a more exposed spot when the weather is fine and mild. Anyway, watering should be limited, as overwatering when it is warmer will lead to excessive budding (bad for bonsai), which then calls for early pinching out. Do not use fertilizer until you are sure the plant has started its growing period, as this would cause the tree to grow too quickly, with the same effects as excessive watering.

Most trees should be pruned for shape before they start growing (usually during the first three weeks of early spring). It is not a good time to do wiring, as the sap on deciduous trees should be flowing freely before they are wired.

If you have some shelter (a cold frame or even better a greenhouse), early spring is the ideal time for seed-raising. In good conditions, the seeds will take a few weeks to come up, taking advantage of the milder mid- and late spring weather to germinate and grow. For all early flowering plants, such as jasmine, now is the time to cut away all faded blooms. Any of these which are left on the tree could encourage fungal disease. It is also a good time for grafting.

The absence of leaves makes wiring easier. Make sure the wires do not mark the bark.

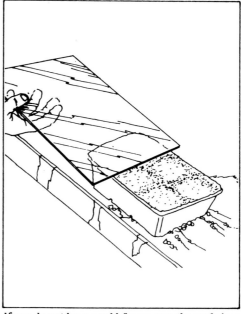

If you do not have a cold-frame, sow the seeds in a dish instead. Cover the dish with a sheet of glass, propped open slightly.

MID-SPRING

If plant growth is too rapid, do not hesitate to pinch out conifer buds.

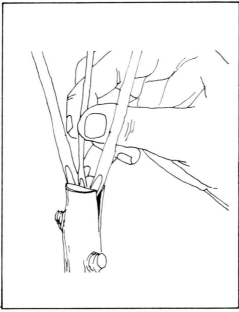

Now is a suitable time for cleft grafting. Do not forget to seal the graft with mastic before binding it to help protect it from diseases.

This is a period of intense growth, (particularly in northern regions), though there is still a risk of frost, especially during the earlier part of this period. However, a drop in temperature will no longer freeze the soil ball through – but the more tender outdoor trees must still be protected.

The earliest weeks of mid-spring are considered to be the best time for transplanting conifers, though it is usually too late for deciduous kinds, which are by then in full growth. It is also an excellent time for grafting, particularly for cleft grafting conifers.

Spring-blooming shrubs are at their best, ablaze with colourful flowers. As in early spring be sure to cut away all dead blooms whenever necessary. As soon as the shrubs have lost all their flowers, they can be pruned to shape. Do not delay pruning, which must be carried out before new buds appear, as blooms are always borne on the previous year's wood. Any delay in pruning will stop them blooming the next year.

If the season is particularly mild, try to limit over-rapid growth by restricting watering, the use of fertilizers, and by pinching out if necessary. Late in mid-spring is also a good time to lift outdoor conifers. It is also time to start transplanting in northern regions, provided the soil has thawed out completely.

This is a good time to repot conifers (before they start into growth) and also to prune their roots.

Mid-spring, like early spring, is a good time for seed-raising. If the seeds are sown in pots in a cold frame, ensure that they are exposed to the air as soon as they begin to sprout, but to shade them from strong sunshine. Seeds and seedlings should be watered moderately, as overwatering in a confined area could set off damping-off disease which quickly kills the young plants.

LATE SPRING

While late spring is certainly a peak period for flowering shrubs, it is the season when bonsai spring back to life with the start of the summer (although there is the risk of a late frost).

Some kinds with delicate leaves (maples, for instance) must be protected against scorching sun, which can easily damage the young shoots.

Be more attentive to watering, in view of the rising temperatures and increased sunshine. This does not mean drowning the plants at the first sign of the soil becoming dry. Excessive watering only leads to over-rapid growth of shoots and larger leaves or needles. Moderate watering will produce smaller leaves and shorter needles.

The same applies to fertilizers. Over-use of fertilizers causes too much growth too rapidly. Deciduous trees require more care than conifers. For a good stimulant, liquid fertilizers are best.

The development of new growth makes late spring the first suitable time for pinching shoots and clipping leaves. The buds of conifers in particular should be reduced, while the leaves of deciduous kinds can be clipped until mid-summer.

Special care must be taken of flowering shrubs of the heather family, like rhododendrons and azaleas, as their dead flowers must be removed. This is a delicate operation which must be carried out when the seeds start to form and not when the blooms start to wither. Care must be taken not to cut the young shoots which are beginning to grow at the base of the pistil and which will eventually carry the next year's flowers. Later, these shoots' growth will have to be kept in check to make sure they do not spoil the shape of the tree. A choice will have to be made between a profusion of flowers and the shape of the bonsai. Measured use of fertilizers will help these plants as they start to make new growth.

From late spring onwards, flowering shrubs of the heather family like azalea and rhododendron burst into full bloom. As soon as the blooms wither, cut them off. You must be very careful not to damage the side shoots. It is the side shoots which will bear next year's flowers.

EARLY SUMMER

The abundant shoots of this juniper must be pinched out in early summer. The softest of them are easily removed with the fingers.

The end of spring is marked by intense growth of foliage, resulting from the great development of the shoots. This must be restrained by frequently inspecting the plants and pinching them even to the extent of pruning away the leaves altogether. This helps miniaturize the next generation of leaves.

With more sun, more attention should be given to watering, which in some circumstances will have to be done several times a day.

Light plays a direct part in shoot development, so it is necessary to turn outdoor bonsai regularly to avoid any imbalance in the branches which would be tricky to rectify later.

Vigorous growth makes early summer the ideal time for certain types of grafts, notably cleft and crown grafts, particularly on conifers.

Most deciduous trees can be wired in early or mid-summer.

Excessively long shoots on deciduous trees must be pruned. Here, special tree scissors with large handles are being used to make accurate cuts.

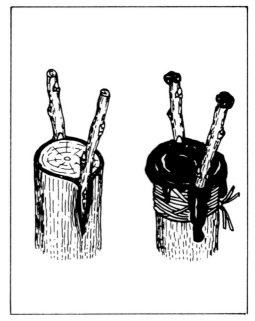

Crown grafting gives excellent results at this time of the year, providing of course, subjects suitable for bonsai are chosen.

MID- TO LATE SUMMER

This is usually the hottest part of the year, so watering is all-important. When the weather is very dry, water twice a day, early in the morning and late at night. In exceptionally hot weather, plants can be watered as often as necessary if their root balls dry out quickly. Take care not to wet the foliage facing the sun as the drops of water can form magnifying glasses, scorching leaves.

To limit evaporation and transpiration from the leaves, it is sometimes necessary to shade bonsai. Their root balls can also be protected with moss, or other materials, such as pine bark, which can be spread evenly round the base of the plant to limit evaporation.

Hot, humid, stormy weather encourages the spread of pests (particularly greenfly) and gives rise to some fungal diseases (such as powdery mildew and rust). So it is important to inspect trees regularly and treat any troubles immediately. Regular watering is essential.

Summer is favourable to plant propagation, and particularly layering and taking cuttings. Take great care with watering young plants raised from spring-sown seeds. Rapid drying out usually kills them.

The use of fertilizers can be reduced, as it is not necessary to encourage growth at this stage. In fact, as growth is vigorous, it is essential to continue pinching as often as is necessary to check the trees' growth.

Summer-flowering trees will have to be tidied up as the blooms wither. This period is often followed by a strong growth of shoots which must be immediately pinched out. This time, there is no fear of damaging the next crop of flowers, as it will be borne on the current year's wood and therefore the shoots made next spring. Pruning these trees and shrubs for shape should not be done now, however, but during the winter.

The full summer sun can be too much for some outdoor bonsai. Watch the watering and, if necessary, shade the more delicate trees.

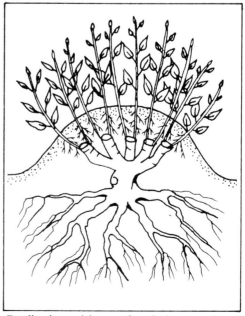

Stooling is a quick way of producing a number of plants which will be almost exactly identical to the parent plant.

EARLY AUTUMN

The time is now perfect for taking cuttings. To facilitate rooting, coat the base of each cutting with hormone rooting powder.

Temperatures and sunlight are gradually decreasing. But it is still necessary to keep an eye on the plants' watering needs, as we can get some very hot days. Keep layers watered so they are ready to be separated from their parent before the next spring.

This is a particularly good time to take cuttings from conifers and to transplant them. Adult plants should be cleared of their yellowing needles.

Autumn is the time to start using fertilizers again to boost the plants' diet ready for winter.

Pinching is no longer necessary, as the shoots have stopped growing.

Treatment against insects and fungi should be continued, as the warm, stormy late summer days particularly encourage greenfly and fungal diseases, such as blight and powdery mildew.

It also pays to protect fruits against attack by birds and wasps.

Place the cutting in a small pot (here of plastic), firm the compost with the thumbs to hold the shoot in place and water well.

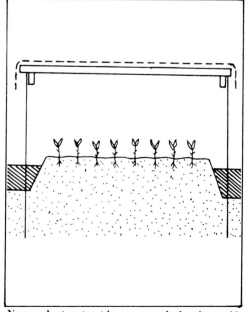

Young plants set out in a nursery bed or in a cold-frame should be shaded from the sun with some temporary shading such as blinds, slats or netting.

MID-AUTUMN

Mid-autumn is marked by a gradual slowing down and eventual cessation of growth, the maturing of fruits and the falling of the leaves.

This is the time when deciduous trees look their best, maple trees taking on magnificent flame red leaf tints.

This gradual ceasing of activity makes it possible to collect and repot plants, particularly deciduous trees, conifers being best transplanted in spring.

Fertilizers can be applied throughout the mid-autumn period.

Also continue tidying up conifers by removing the old needles. About half way through this period, the first night frosts can be expected, so it is time to start protecting the most tender plants. Do this either by bringing them into a cool, well ventilated room or by covering them at night.

Watering will depend on the weather, as the warm autumn sun can still dry out the root ball. Avoid spraying the foliage, as this is no longer useful and could even be harmful, as it tends to encourage fungal diseases.

Fruit trees (particularly apple trees) are at the peak of fruiting, enhancing the autumn foliage tints. Towards the end of this period, the ripe fruits will start to fall. They should not be left on top of the root ball, as they could give rise to fungal diseases as they decompose. For the same reason, dead leaves that fall from the trees should be swept away. Though it is too late to graft deciduous trees, it is still possible to graft conifers throughout the dormant period. Gradually reduce watering of the cuttings kept in a greenhouse or a cold frame and pot up those which are well rooted.

Start stratifying any tree seeds with hard shells. Spread them in pots of damp sand in a cold place, at the foot of a wall for instance. Wherever you place them, make sure there is no risk of frost.

Deciduous trees are starting to take on their magnificent autumn tints. Sweep away any leaves that fall on the root ball.

Fruit trees are . . . fruiting! It is remarkable that the tiny fruits (here crab apples) are in scale with the bonsai – a miracle of nature!

LATE AUTUMN

Some impressive equipment used for wiring trees. *From left to right*: wire cutters, branch cutters and scissors. Keep them sharp.

Now the leaves of this weeping willow have fallen, it is time to check and correct the wiring which was carried out in the summer.

Winter is approaching and the leaves are dropping quickly now, except for the beeches, which retain their leaves for most of the winter, dropping their dead leaves only when the young shoots start to sprout.

Remember to protect or bring in any tender bonsai, as the first serious frosts can be anticipated during the later part of this period. Bringing them in does not mean putting these plants in a heated frame or greenhouse, which would only disrupt their cycle of growth. They should be stood in a cool, well-lit, well-ventilated place, where the temperature never rises above 6–8°C (43–46°F).

When the leaves drop, carefully examine the bark on the branches and trunk for any signs of greenfly or larvae. If you find any of these pests, scrape the bark and check as well any bends in the tree and places where it was pruned the previous year. Any bark which is in poor condition should be removed with a jin scalpel (see page 68) and the scar covered in mastic.

Pruning for shape can start in late autumn, particularly on deciduous trees, though it should be limited to correcting the smaller growth, leaving any major work on the branches until the end of winter. Winter is the period just before the tree starts to grow again.

Stop giving fertilizer at the end of the late autumn period.

Reduce the amount of water you give, as the plant no longer needs much. By soaking the soil, you will only encourage fungal diseases, especially on the roots.

From now on conifers can be wired, which is an essential part of bonsai training. Do not wrap the wire too tightly otherwise the bark may be marked when growth starts again.

Protect young layers against frost by mulching or mounding and protect any cuttings left in a cold-frame.

EARLY WINTER

With winter upon us, all bonsai trees vulnerable to severe frost should have been taken indoors or given some form of protection from the cold. If you have nowhere to put any delicate plants, make a temporary wooden or metal frame covered with a lid of transparent plastic (such as a polythene sheet). This has the advantage that it can easily be removed or opened as soon as the temperature rises, so that plants can benefit from the sunlight and good ventilation too.

You can continue wiring conifers to shape them throughout the winter.

Watering should almost cease, to limit the risk of the soil, and therefore the roots, freezing during any unexpectedly early cold snaps. Fertilizer serves no useful purpose in winter, since the plant is dormant and so needs no nutrients.

INDOOR BONSAI

The seasonal cycle of growth of indoor bonsai is very different from that of outdoor bonsai, since there are no seasonal variations in climate. But this is not to say that the plant itself has no seasonal cycle. It is governed by its own biological rhythms, rather than by environmental factors.

Although watering should continue for most of the year (tropical plants not being used to any dry season), fertilizer should not be given in winter.

Pruning for shape should be carried out in early spring, with leaves (of the ficus species, for example) being cut back as spring ends. Wiring can be undertaken all year round, but be sure not to leave wires in position for more than three to six months without removing and adjusting them.

Repotting should take place in spring every second year. The roots should be pruned at the same time and the proportions of the root ball corrected.

GLOSSARY

A

ACAULESCENT A plant without a stem between the roots and the first leaves.

ACCLIMATIZE Adapting a plant to a climate different from that of its native region.

ACIDITY The concentration of acid in the soil (sulphuric, hydrochloric, nitric, etc), measured in terms of pH (an acid soil is 6 or below).

ADVENTITIOUS Part of a plant developing in a place where it would not normally grow; for instance adventitious roots which grow on the stem of ivy.

AFFINITY Physiological similarity between two plants. This is essential when grafting rootstock and scion material.

ALKALINITY The opposite of acidity, usually characterized by soda, lime or ammonia, all alkaline substances. Measured in terms of pH (an alkaline soil registers 7 or above).

ALTERNATE The arrangement of leaves or branches which arise first on one side of the stem and then the other.

ARCHING or ARCURE The curves imposed on the branches by wiring.

ARIL An extra covering around the seed coat. It is red, fleshy and cup shaped in the case of yew, but is a tuft of hairs in willows.

AXIL The angle formed by a lateral branch with the trunk or by a leaf with a branch.

AXILLARY Bud, shoot or flower growing from the axil. The axillary is also known as a lateral bud.

B

BORDEAUX MIXTURE A lime and copper sulphate solution long used as a fungicide.

BUD An embryo shoot, flower or flower cluster, usually protected by scales.

BUDDING A leaf bud, or 'eye', taken with a sliver of bark, which will be grafted on to another plant.

BUSHY The shape of a bush or shrub, which branches from the base rather than having a central stem or trunk, in which case it would be described as tree-like or arborescent.

C

CAMBIUM Actively dividing cell tissue just beneath the bark which is capable of producing new cells, controlling the growth of the wood and bark.

CHLOROSIS A deficiency disease indicated by leaves turning yellow from a lack of chlorophyll, which is in turn due to iron deficiency.

COMPOST A mixture of soil, peat, sand and other materials in varying proportions to suit the requirements of a plant for which it will provide the growing medium.

CONTOURING Building a mound of soil round the base of a plant. Some tender shrubs are mounded in late autumn to protect them from cold, especially in districts where winters are harsh. Contouring the soil round a bonsai enhances its appearance.

CULTIVAR (cv) A plant which has been selected or bred by man. It differs from other individuals of the same species by one or more characteristics which serve to identify the plant type. A cultivar can differ considerably from the species itself by the shape of its leaves or the number and colour of its petals.

CUTTING A technique of reproduction used for propagating plants. Part of a plant (root, branch, bud or leaf) is cut off and rooted to form a new plant. The new plant subsequently reproduces the qualities and defects (diseases for example) of the parent plant.

CUTTING BACK This is the trimming of the foliage and roots of a bonsai plant before repotting or transplanting it into a new container.

D

DAMPING OFF The collapse and death of seedlings or young plants after they have germinated. This is caused by a group of fungi living in the soil or compost. It can be avoided by always using fresh compost for sowing seeds.

DEBUDDING Removing one or a proportion of the buds from a bonsai to limit the number of shoots and therefore leaves that develop when growth begins in spring.

DEGENERATION The progressive deterioration of a plant due to old age or viral disease.

DECIDUOUS The habit of shedding all the leaves annually; a characteristic of many trees and shrubs. The opposite of evergreen.

DIVISION A method of reproducing plants by splitting well-rooted clumps into smaller pieces, each with at least one strong shoot and good root system. Each of these pieces will quickly develop into a new plant.

DORMANT PERIOD A period when a plant rests (often during the winter months or during a period of drought). A dormant period is sometimes induced artificially to speed up growth.

DOWNY MILDEW A disease that mainly attacks vines and potatoes, though also a number of other plants. It shows itself as mouldy patches on the leaves surrounded by a halo. These patches dry out from the centre.

E

ETIOLATION This is a blanching or yellowing of the leaves, caused by lack of light which prevents photosynthesis taking place.

EVERGREEN The characteristic of a plant which retains its leaves beyond the annual cycle of growth. (Many conifers are evergreen). Evergreen means the opposite of deciduous.

F

FIBROUS ROOTS These are the fine capillary feeding roots that develop from the main anchoring roots of a tree.

FOREST A multiple arrangement of bonsai in a single tray to give the illusion of a miniature forest.

FUNGICIDE A chemical product for treating fungal diseases.

G

GALLS These are swollen growths that result from the activity of various parasites. They can also be formed as a defence mechanism by the plant when it has been damaged.

GRAFTING The method of joining together two compatible plants in order to reproduce the qualities of the one in the other; the stock provides the roots and the scion provides the top of the plant with the desired flowering, fruiting or other qualities.

GROWTHS Young branches in the course of development, consisting of shoots and leaves. One must distinguish between shoots that have flowered and those that have not if one is to thin successfully without damaging the plant.

H

HARDY Plants capable of withstanding harsh climatic conditions, especially frost.

HEELING IN Planting temporarily in a trench whilst awaiting final planting when ground is properly prepared, soil is in right condition or container is ready.

I

INSECTICIDE A toxic product used in various forms to kill insects and mites.

IKADA A single tree laid horizontally with vertical branches.

J

JIN A technique of artificially ageing branches and trunks by removing the bark, bleaching with acid and polishing the wood.

L

LAYERING A way of propagating plants which involves encouraging an aerial shoot to form roots, then severing it from the parent to obtain a new plant. Many plants layer themselves naturally.

M

MANURE Fertilizing and soil improving material which will provide the plant with the kind of food that will help it develop. It should only be used when well rotted.

MISTING Damping over plant foliage with a mist of water. A technique used mainly on young plants raised from seed.

MOSAIC A viral disease which seriously depresses growth characterized by mottling of the leaves.

MULCHING This cultivation technique is used to protect plants by covering the surrounding soil, and sometimes the crown of the plant itself. It gives protection from the cold and prevents evaporation of moisture from the soil.

N

NEUTRALITY Chemical state of a soil which is neither acid nor alkaline on the pH scale.

NODE The point of origin, often slightly swollen, of any leaf on a stem.

NURSERY BED An area set aside in a garden for sowing and planting out young plants before they are moved to their final growing positions.

O

OPPOSITE ARRANGEMENT This is quite simply an arrangement of leaves or branches which grow face to face on a branch or trunk.

OVERWINTER To bring plants into the shelter of a greenhouse, a cold-frame or indoors in late autumn to protect them from winter frosts or cold, damp conditions.

P

PARASITE Primarily plants that grow on others and then feed off them, but the term is also used for certain insects and other creatures that prosper to the detriment of the host plant.

PERENNIAL Any plant which lives for several years, unlike an annual which completes its life cycle in one year or a biennial which completes its life cycle in two years.

PESTICIDE A formulation for destroying animal organisms detrimental to plant growth.

pH The scale which is used to measure the acidity or alkalinity of the soil. The soil is said to be neutral if its pH equals 7.0. It is said to be acid if it has a lower pH than this and to be alkaline if it has a higher pH than this. If the acidity of the soil is too high or too low for a particular plant it will not grow well and may die, so it is useful to know the soil's pH.

PHYTOSANITARY A product that favours the healthy development and functioning of a plant by protecting it from pests and diseases.

PINCHING Nipping out certain young shoots with the finger nails in order to limit growth and therefore any irregular development of the plant.

PRUNING The removal (with secateurs or a saw) of shoots or branches which are old, diseased, damaged or unwanted, in order to stimulate new shoots.

PUDDLING Dipping the roots of a shrub in a slurry of soil, water and possibly other nutritious materials to help the subject, when planted, establish itself quickly and strongly. Cow dung is often mixed with heavy clay soil.

R

RADICAL In horticultural terms, this means pertaining to the roots.

ROOT ROT A fungus disease that takes the form of a mould that attacks the roots of a tree and eventually rots them away. It often results from putting fresh manure straight on the roots.

ROOTSTOCK A plant used in propagation by grafting to provide support, control vigour and receive the scion. For the graft to take, the rootstock and scion must be compatible, otherwise the scion will be rejected. It is not possible to graft a conifer on to a hardwood or to graft a hardwood on to a conifer.

S

SCION A part of a plant with desirable qualities, eg flowering, fruiting, with attractive form, but a poor or unsatisfactory rooting characteristic, which can be grafted on to the rootstock of a similar plant.

SEED SOWING Quite simply the method of reproducing plants sexually by germinating seeds.

SPECIES (spp.) A group of individual plants that exhibit the same distinctive characteristics. It is the plant unit that provides the basis for classification.

STEM The aerial part of a plant which carries the leaves.

STERILIZATION Destruction of harmful organisms, fungal spores, weed seeds, etc, in soil or compost by means of heat or chemicals.

STOCK *see* Rootstock.

STRATIFICATION A way of preparing seeds to soften or crack their protective shell so as to break their dormancy and make germination possible. Seeds to be stratified are spread in layers of damp sand in a cold place throughout the winter, protected from mice and other predators that could eat them.

SUCKER Underground stem growing from the roots of a plant which can be used for propagation.

T

TRANSPLANTING Moving a plant to its final position where it can develop fully. A plant can be moved several times to strengthen its root system.

TRAY A shallow or flat container, often glazed externally, which is used for growing bonsai.

V

VIRAL DISEASE A disease caused by the sub-microscopic particles called viruses. These weaken and distort the plant. Any plant suffering from viral disease should be burnt so that it does not affect other plants and should never be used for propagation purposes.

W

WIRING Method of training a tree, by wrapping a metal wire (usually copper) around trunk or branches to produce a predetermined shape.

INDEX

D

damping off (seedlings) 30, 35–6
date palm 14
deciduous trees 86–7, **109**
  choosing 102
  disbudding 57
  leaf trimming 57
  pinching 58, **59**, 87
  transplanting 28
  wiring 64, 106
dehydration *see* watering
debudding 57
diseases 98–100, 103, 107, 108, 109
  preventing when sowing 30, 31
display 83, **83**

E

elm **12**, **59**, 62
English method (grafting) **51**
equipment *see* tools

F

Fagus 62
  crenata 87
false acacia **10**
false cypress **12**, **25**, **38**, 85
feeding 79–80
fertilizers 79–80, **79**, **80**, 99
  autumn use 108, 109, 110
  indoor plants 91
  root rot 100, 102
  spring use 103, 104, 105
  summer use 107
Ficus **39**, **90**, 92
fig **39**, **82**, **82**, **90**, 92
fir 85
firethorn 62, **88**, 89
flowers 12
foliage *see* leaves
foliar feeds 80
forests (Yose Ue) 24–5, **24**, **25**, 70
frost 83, 102, 103, 104, 109, 110, 111
fruit trees 109
  pruning 62
fruits 12, **12**
Fukinagashi 20, **21**, 24

fungal diseases 98–9, 103, 107, 108, 109

G

Gardenia jasminoiides 92
germination of seeds 29–35
Ginqko biloba 87
glossary 112–15
grafting:
  error correction 54
  propagation by 46–51, 103, 104
grass 95
greenfly 95, 96, **96**, 107
greenhouses **36**, 45, 82
grey bark elm **86**, 87

H

Han-kengaï 20, **21**
hawthorn 89
heel cuttings 37–8
hermaphrodite plants 12
hibiscus 82
history of bonsai 16–17, **17**
Hôkidachi 20, **21**, 24
holly **29**
hornbeam **86**, 87
horse chestnut **10**
house plant care products, caution
  needed with 80

I

Ikada Buki **22**, 23
indoor bonsai 78, **82**, 90–2, 111
insect larvae 95, 97
Ishitzuki 20, **21**, 24

J

Japan and bonsai 16–25, 27, 54, 70
Japanese apricot 89
Japanese black pine 62
Japanese camellia 92
Japanese cherry 89
Japanese grey bark elm **86**, 87
Japanese maple **60**
Jasminum nudiflorum 89